Introduction

John O'Brien & Connie Lyle O'Brien

Through person-centered planning's first eighteen years, its early developers have been busy doing plans with people and their families, guiding others in learning to facilitate planning, consulting with organizations and systems exploring person-centered work, and joining people with disabilities and their families to tell participants in conferences and workshops about what they have learned. They have written how-to manuals to support their training and consultation and a number of monographs and book chapters on applications of person-centered planning to specific groups of people and to efforts to change organizations and policies (the reference section in Chapter 14 includes a bibliography of many of these materials and contact addresses for locating them).

Interest in person-centered planning has grown rapidly over the past few years, both reflecting and driving growth in numbers of practitioners and variety of methods and sponsors among technical assistance organizations. This growth in interest has shaped policy in the several authorities and many agencies that have adopted person-centered planning as a method of choice for at least some of the groups of people they serve. Policies in turn have increased the number of technical assistants, trainings and manuals available. Only recently has interest in person-centered planning extended into published efforts to investigate some of its practices and, in a far more limited way, its effects on people's futures (see, for example, Fox, Vaughn, Dunlap & Bucey, 1997; Hagner, Helm, & Butterworth, 1996; Miner & Bates 1977; Whitney-Thomas, Shaw, Honey, & Butterworth, 1998).

How this book happened (and some of the people who will shape the next volume)

This little book was born at the copy machine. In addition to several manuals and monographs, early developers of person-centered planning have written a number of pieces about person-centered planning. (Usually shorter) versions of some of these have found their way into newsletters and chapters of books published on other topics, but as interest grows so does time deciding what to send to people who inquire about person centered planning. A colleague wrote an appreciative recommendation for person-centered planning in which he said that his biggest frustration was tracking down materials that were circulated widely in n^{th} generation copies but published, if at all, in workshop handouts and newsletters and books that are hard to find. Another colleague noted that people who learn one approach to person-centered planning often have limited exposure to the materials that circulate among practitioners of other approaches. This little book is our best current answer to the question, "What should I read about person-centered planning if I want to know more about the beliefs that shape it; about its assumptions and its limits and its proper use?"

We invited Beth Mount, Michael Smull, Marsha Forest and Jack Pearpoint, and Judith Snow to join us in contributing short pieces that they think it important for people practicing person-centered planning to read and think about. The work of Herb Lovett, whose untimely death kept him from participating more directly, is represented in Chapter 14. Everyone interested in person-centered planning should read his *Learning to listen* (1996) for an echo of the thoughtfully compassionate, sometimes brilliant, sometimes quirky, sometimes infuriating force that Herb brought to planning with people whose behavior is difficult, whether or not they are disabled,

Each chapter was written at a different time and for different purposes, and we have resisted the temptation to rewrite them, except for adding PATH to the brief descriptions of different approaches in Chapter 14 and minor editing of Chapter 12. It is possible to use the papers here to trace a history of person centered planning. For example, Chapter 16, written in 1984, reads a bit strangely to us now. Its perspective casts person-centered planning more as a procedure to be done to people, with their consent, than as a way to walk with people through changes in their lives. The key ideas of focusing on people's gifts and consciously forming support circles are unformed. It is more optimistic about the ability of organizations to use person-centered planning than experience has made us.

There are many other committed and thoughtful practitioners whose important variations of person-centered planning forge new tools and take the work into new contexts. We think of Susannah Joyce's creative gathering and telling the stories of changes facilitated by person-centered planning; the nexus of projects animated by Helen Sanderson in the Northwest of England and the staff of SHS in Scotland; the work of Bill Allen and John Shea and their associates with California's Regional Centers and Rehabilitation agency;

A little book about

PERSON CENTERED PLANNING

EDITED BY　　　　　　**Volume I**

JOHN O'BRIEN & CONNIE LYLE O'BRIEN

INCLUSION PRESS

Canadian Cataloguing in Publication Data

O'Brien, John 1946
A Little Book About Person-Centred Planning
© Responsive Systems Associates Inc., 1998. All Rights Reserved
Includes index.
ISBN 1-895418-40-2

I. Handicapped - Services for. I. O'Brien, John, 1946 -
II. O'Brien, Connie Lyle. III Forest, Marsha, 1942-2000
Pearpoint, Jack, 1945-

HV1568.L.57 1998   362.4   C98-932448-6

Fourth Printing – 2007

Published by *Inclusion Press*
                24 Thome Crescent
                Toronto, Ontario M6H 2S5
                Canada

Preparation of this book was partially supported through a subcontract to Responsive Systems Associates from the Center on Human Policy, Syracuse University for the Research and Training Center on Community Living. The Research and Training Center on Community Living is supported through a cooperative agreement (number H133B30072) between the National Institute on Disability & Rehabilitation Research (NIDRR) and the University of Minnesota Institute on Community Integration. Members of the Center are encouraged to express their opinions; these do not necessarily represent the official position of NIDRR.

Cover design: Catherine Hollands
Cover photograph: © Jack Pearpoint, Mach Pichu, Peru

Contents

the efforts to bring person-centered planning to people with trau-
matic brain injury undertaken by the Research and Training Center
at Mount Siani Hospital; the methodical, long-term work of
Caroline Bardwell Wheeler and Hope Leet Dittmeier to shape
much needed expansion of Kentucky's system through planning that
begins in their own personal commitments; Rebecca Shuman and
Myrna Bartlett's and Claudia Bolton and Becky Donofrio's integration of person-centered planning into supported living in Michigan
and California; the Institute for Community Inclusion's development of and research on Whole Life Planning; the thoughtful and
careful ways people associated with Ohio Safeguards and the ARC
of Ohio have helped people uncover their personal and family auto-
biographies and point to a brighter future; the Beach Center on
Families and Disability's Group Action Planning, which links person-centered planning with the lives of young children and their
families; Sally Sehmsdorf and Mary Romer's exploration of ways to
enlist and support citizens from outside disability services as facilitators of planning and action; the links between person-centered
planning and community building guided throughout Pennsylvania
by the Support Circle Mentoring Project and in Philadelphia by the
Friendship Project; Anne Malatchi and her colleagues' systematic
approach to changing schools through person-centered planning;
Patty Cotton and Jo Ann Sowers' extensions of person-centered
planning into service-brokerage in New Hampshire's evolving system; and Gina Gross and Bruce Anderson's creation of ways to draw
on the deeper forces that shape community in planning and searching for better futures with people. We know there are many other
creative practitioners we have not yet had the chance to meet. Their
reflections on their own work would add much to the papers gathered here, and we hope to sample and share the thoughts of other
creative practitioners in a future volume, which will be a not so little
book about person-centered planning.

Some themes
Because this little book includes reflections about person-centered
planning there is more common ground among its chapters than a
book that collected descriptions of how different contributors conduct the process of person-centered planning would have. Indeed,
anyone who reads the book straight through will find redundancy of
central ideas in the orientation of people who sometimes are seen by
others as promoting competing schools of person-centered plan-

ning. Awareness of this redundancy seems to us to be no bad thing. Some of the threads that tie the chapters together include these.

Person-centered planning celebrates, relies on, and finds its sober hope in people's interdependence. At its core, it is a vehicle for people to make worthwhile, and sometimes life changing, promises to one another.

Person-centered planning aims to expand the power that people have to choose life conditions and experiences that make sense for them. This makes it an important source of insight into the meaning of choice for people who rely on others who are paid with public money to assist them. This insight drives practitioners to appreciate imposed constraints as motivators for creative, and occasionally even daring, problem solving.

People are best understood in terms of their contributions, personal interests, and gifts. The way a community regards people with disabilities typically inhibits the discovery and expression of a person's contributions to the common good. Practitioners take a stand for people's gifts. A person's experience of disability can inhibit discovery and expression of personal interests and contributions. So, when specialist knowledge and skill is relevant to decreasing barriers, practitioners of person-centered planning help people and their circles of support build a strong context for creative professional work.

Person-centered planning begins when people decide to listen carefully and in ways that can strengthen the voice of people who have been or are at risk of being silenced. Willingness to join in action toward a desirable future tests the depth and accuracy of listening.

Person-centered planning raises, and can productively contain, many difficult ethical issues. Some of these issues arise around negotiating support for people's choices; others around protecting vulnerable people from threats to their well-being; others around the proper use of one's energy and talents in relation to systems that may be poorly prepared to support a person and poorly motivated for the deep change that offering good support would require. Practitioners have an obligation to be thoughtful and courageous about when and how they plan with people.

The processes of person-centered planning can be powerful, but they are ordinary. Practitioners need to feel the effects of these processes in their own lives, by making plans for themselves with their own circles of support, however those circles may be shaped. Practitioners owe it to the people they serve to personally exemplify courage in defining their own dreams and recruiting other's support to pursue them. They also accept responsibility for making a continuing investment in improving their own understanding, knowledge, and abilities as listeners, as facilitators, as organizers, and as learners through reflection-in-action.

Person-centered planning embodies different ideas about disability, support, and community than most human service programs and policies do in practice, though the stated aspirations of many service organizations have caught up. This tension between aspiration and capacity can either energize significant organizational change or drive organizations to deny the contradictions that person-centered planning surfaces. If it is not a source of considerable tension with typical practice and power relationships, person-centered planning may have been tamed past real usefulness. Practitioners should be a conscious part of efforts to change the social situation of the people they plan with, either as part of a planned effort to change existing service patterns from within or in alliances dedicated to changing systems from outside. They should expect –and find strategic ways to resist– predictable efforts to embody conflicting ideas in person-centered planning –for example, recent attempts to define (and then to regulate) person-centered planning as a variety of professional counselling or to define person-centered planning, in itself, as a sort of therapeutic intervention whose efficacy can be tested as if it were a drug.

Person-centered planning faces a challenge of growth in scale. Developing system and organizational capacity to move from few to many thoughtfully implemented person-centered plans confronts common understandings of how, and how easily, systems and organizations transform themselves.

Planning alone does not change people's lives. Person-centered planning offers people who want to make change a forum for discovering shared images of a desirable future, negotiating conflicts, doing creative problem solving, making and checking agreements on action, refining direction while adapting action to changing situations, and offering one another mutual support. But without people working together in a sustained and careful way in the world outside the planning circle, change can not happen. Most of the discussion of supporting structures in this book concerns the people who form a person's closest circle of support. For one way of understanding the implications of person-centered planning for organizing supports see our discussion of the networks of relationships and agreements necessary to deliver effective support (O'Brien, Lyle O'Brien, & Jacob, 1998).

Many people with disabilities and their families testify to the promise of person centered planning (see for example, Joyce, 1993 and Joyce, 1996). Realizing this promise for growing numbers of people will take both skill with the tools of person-centered planning and thought about the ethics and strategies for these tools' proper use. We hope this little book will help those who facilitate person-centered plans to develop their own ideas about how best to use their talents.

We would welcome additional written reflections on the practice of person-centered planning; contact us at 58 Willowick Drive, Lithonia, GA 30038-1722 (e-mail 72263.3724@compuserve.com).

References

Fox, L., Vaughn, B., Dunlap, G. & Bucey, M. (1997). Parent-professional partnership in behavioral support: A qualitative analysis of one family's experience. *JASH 22*(4), 198-217.

Hagner, D., Helm, D, & Butterworth, J. (1996). "This is your meeting": A qualitative study of person-centered planning. *Mental Retardation 34*(3), 159-171

Joyce, S. (1993). *Collage: Stories of a circle of support.* London, ON: Realizations.

Joyce, S. (1996). *Samplings: Seven stories of personal planning.* London, ON: Realizations.

Lovett, H. (1996). *Learning to listen: Positive approaches and people with difficult behavior.* Baltimore: Paul Brookes Publishing.

Miner, C. & Bates P. (1997). The effects of person-centered planning activities on the IEP/transition planning process. *Education and Training in Mental Retardation and Developmental Disabilities 32*(2), 105-112.

O'Brien, Lyle O'Brien, C. & Jacob, G. (1998). *Celebrating everyday life: The emergence of Options in Community Living as a thoughtful organization.* Toronto: Inclusion Press.

Whitney-Thomas, J., Shaw, D., Honey, K., & Butterworth, J. (1998). Building a future: A study of student participation in person centered planning. *JASH 23*(2), 119-133.

The Power In Vulnerability

Judith A. Snow

We often think of human life as residing in individual bodies. We think about each other as if I were a Thing and you were a Thing and we two Things interact now and then, all the while remaining separate entities. This is not a very powerful model for describing how our lives are sustained or how we in fact develop our capacity to contribute to each other and to our society at large.

I believe that it is more powerful to think about human life as if it were a thread floating between and connecting bodies –giving each body the capacity to be a person. Alone I am alive but not revealed or fulfilled. In relationship with one person I am able to become the qualities that the relationship allows for. For example in relationship with my mother I am enabled to be a child, a student, a loved one, a potential caregiver as she becomes older, and much more.

When I come into relationship with two people I acquire the capacity to become more than twice of what I am with one person. The presence of both individuals to each other creates possibilities that don't exist with each alone with me. For example my mother and my mother's friend each see me as a very different person, drawing different capacities from me. My mother and her friend together create their own new possibilities in the world and, connected with me, we create yet even more possibilities of me, more than either one does with me alone.

As an individual's relationships increase in number and diversity the possibilities for that person give great room for that person to both become themselves and draw forth new capacity in others. In other words one or two threads will offer little support but a gossamer network of even five or six threads has strength to sustain a rich life.

Euthanasia and other Sanctity of Life questions are raised very often these days when people with disabilities are being talked about. The focus of discussion is inevitably on the person's physical and cognitive functioning. The concern is to determine a benchmark of capacity that would allow experts to say with certainty when it is appropriate to end a "damaged" life. But physical and cognitive functioning are virtually no more than a necessary condition for life. In the presence of a body from human parents –breathing, if only assisted by a respirator– I am in the presence of the first essential for human life. The condition of having a breathing body really only sets a background for me to have capacity.

When I am in relationship with other individuals and if these others are networked with each other and especially if these others are different from each other, the possibility exists for all of us to have a rich life, drawing on each other's gifts. Differences in each other's physical and cognitive functioning, our interests, history and experience, our possessions and resources only add to the mix of possibilities that increase our total capacity.

Many people, especially parents of a newly labeled child, establish their relationship with a person who is handicapped through a process of identifying a need the person is struggling with or through empathizing with an experience of injustice that the person is undergoing. Taking on the role of therapist and advocate, one person stands by the other.

Therapy calls for the person with a handicap to be seen as needing to be fixed in some way. Advocacy calls for the person with a handicap to be viewed as a victim of some outrageous misfortune or circumstance. Both these stances have value and can lead to good for the person and the community. But neither approach calls for a contribution from the labeled person in order to sustain the relationship or the work. And if success in therapy or advocacy is not quickly forthcoming the relationship must suffer. Paradoxically even success can destroy such a relationship because success erodes its foundation.

Sustained vibrant relationship demands that the person with a handicap be viewed with a different vision and listened to with a different ear. Foremost of the alternative possibilities is to see and hear the person as a welcome fellow traveler. We must see our shared life journey as one of transforming human suffering by creating the supportive relationships we all need to sustain life and of celebrating together life's joys, victories and surprises.

As fellow participants in an imperfect community many persons with disabilities have valuable gifts to offer. Some show a capacity to take a great deal of satisfaction from very simple everyday occurrences. The unusual behavior of others can be a contribution to those who find society's restricted codes too tight for self-expression. The silent ones may be the best listeners. The very presence of many people with handicaps is a means out of the overwhelming individualism imposed by society's norms. Then there is an unlimited number of possible gifts that individually each person with a handicap can develop, like everyone, the nature of which can only be determined by those who stand close enough to watch, listen, care and share.

Welcoming into community those who have been excluded and recreating community so that these people's giftedness becomes part of everyday life – this is the strong road to building the capacity of communities everywhere.

Learning to Listen

John O'Brien & Connie Lyle O'Brien

*Listen with an intensity
that most people
save for talking.*
–Lilly Tomlin's
"Edith Ann"

What does it mean to listen?

People come to life when they make contact with someone who works actively and faithfully to understand what they want to say. When people communicate in unconventional ways, or when they have been rendered invisible by an environment that discounts the worth of their communication, the effects of listening can be profoundly energizing. Those who communicate without words, those who use words and symbols in unique ways, and those who communicate within the drama of their behavior call on their listeners' whole emotional, mental, and spiritual selves. They remind us that listening is much more than passing strings of words from mouth to ear. Listening is resonating in body, in imagination, and in spirit. Listening to people who live with the consequences of a lifetime of isolation and discrimination is often painful, frightening, and exciting.

Listening liberates energy. A person's sense of direction grows stronger. The possibility of conflict with established rules, common practices, and fixed views of the person's possibilities increases. Blocked listening generates frustration. To want to understand and not to get the message can lead to a sense of impotence and anger.

As interest in person-centered planning grows, the refrain, "listen to the person," becomes almost too familiar. Being able to say how important it is to listen is not the same as listening actively and faithfully to people who are just finding their voice. To improve our ability to listen, it is important to examine three dimensions of our listening: where we listen from, what we listen for, and how we listen.

Where we listen from We listen best when we stand with people; close enough to smell and hear each other, to touch and be touched. Standing with a person means being willing to accommodate the person's preferences for communicating, and being willing to thoughtfully consider joining the person in taking action. Habit tempts us to stand over or stand away from people with disabilities. In many agencies, informal norms encourage staff to keep "them" under control to minimize liability or to maintain routines. We stand over people when we expect them to tell us their dreams at times and places and in terms that are comfortable for us. Much training promotes detachment and "objectivity". We stand away from people when we collect data to map their lives into our categories –whether that data accounts frequencies of target behaviors or visions of a desirable future. Frustration or conflict evokes habits of control or distance. These habits take us away from the question we most need to answer. "How can I show this person that I want to join her; that I want to be on her side in a constructive way. Maybe I won't be able to help her do what she wants, but I want her to know that understanding what she wants matters to me."

What we listen for We listen best when we encourage people to find their voice. Individualism distorts our understanding of voice into a solo performance: one person clamoring to put himself first. A better understanding recognizes that voice serves participation and contribution. Voice grows in social context, as a person discovers what he wants to say, develops a way to communicate it, and knows that others care to hear and respond. Listening is not about granting wishes; it is a matter of attending to the details and dreams that disclose a person's identity and desires to participate and contribute. As people develop their voice, their sense of their individual place in their world grows more particular, more complex, and more strong. Sometimes a developing voice becomes shrill or cracks before a person can sound true notes; sometimes it isn't easy or pleasant to hear what a person has to express as they find their way through difficult or self-defeating situations. (For wonderful descriptions of the way people with developmental disabilities create lives with those who hear and confirm their voices, see Taylor, Bogdan, & Lutfiyya, 1995.)

How we listen We listen best when we listen with care. Care is not feeling pity. It is attending to the threads of meaning that emerge from thoughtful investigation of a person's biography, discerning expressions of competence, interest, concern, and passion in her responses to day-to-day experience, and creating invitations for considered discussion of her dreams. Care means acknowledging vulnerabilities, fears, disappointments, and failures and the ways a person understands these experiences and finds the courage to keep on. Care expresses an active interest in taking the person's point of view and seeing how her actions make sense to her, even when they seem discordant or opaque to others.

Slowed down and described this way, listening may seem like an activity for a few saints. What is hopeful is how many people have the gift of listening and how many people can discover and refine this gift when they allow people with developmental disabilities to be their teachers. What is challenging is to manage service organizations in such a way that their staff feel encouraged to listen and the people with disabilities who use them feel encouraged to find and develop their own voices.

How can agency managers promote listening?

Managers promote listening to people with disabilities when they build a culture of listening. Effective managers…

… themselves practice listening to people with disabilities, often as a member of one or more circles of support

… encourage a climate of listening among staff, beginning with their own practice of listening deeply and respectfully to their own staff

… challenge formal policies and informal practices that encourage staff to stand over or to stand away from the people they support and actively encourage staff to stand with the people they support

… strongly encourage organizational openness to the many different people who can make a positive contribution to people's future; this often means creatively negotiating conflicts between people with disabilities and members of their families or between staff who want to support a person and representatives of regulatory authorities

… increase organizational flexibility to use agency resources in supporting constructive responses to the dreams and aspirations of people with disabilities, in practice this has involved everything from allowing exceptions to policy to completely restructuring the agency and its programs

Listening requires the personal courage to be open and sensitive to situations that can be difficult and confusing. Leading an organization of listeners requires the wisdom to develop the capacity to take direction from the people the agency exists to serve. A culture of listening increases an agency's capacity to enable people to serve one another in a way that would meet the test that Robert K. Greenleaf (1977) set for leadership:

> *Do those served*
> *grow as persons;*
> *do they,*
> *while being served,*
> *become healthier,*
> *wiser, freer,*
> *more autonomous,*
> *more likely themselves*
> *to become servants?*

References

Greenleaf, R. (1977) *Servant leadership.* Mahwah, NJ: Paulist Press.

Taylor, S., Bogdan, R., & Lutfiyya, Z.M. (1995). *The varieties of community experience.* Baltimore, MD: Paul Brookes Publishers.

Person-centered Planning Has Arrived... or Has It?

Connie Lyle O'Brien, John O'Brien & Beth Mount

Person-centered planning has arrived. A number of states endorse its use in reforming their systems and several require it, at least for members of protected classes; seminars thrive; some officials wonder about certifying person-centered planners; proponents argue the relative advantages of a growing number of methods; researchers call for studies to quantify its effects; critics of service fads joke sarcastically about many-colored markers and little stick people; and, perhaps most tellingly, person-centered planning has acquired an acronym, and now it seems like almost everyone is "doing PCP". At this point it's worth wondering where person-centered planning has arrived and what might get lost as the rate of adoption climbs.

As participants in the early and continuing development of person-centered planning, we've become interested in what happens to a good idea when it moves into mainstream use. We agree with Ellen Langer that an idea's utility lasts only as long as people apply it mindfully, and that any tool's power can be diluted or even misdirected by its mindless use. As Langer distinguishes these orientations,

> *A mindful approach to any activity has three characteristics: the continuous creation of new categories; openness to new information; and an implicit awareness of more than one perspective. Mindlessness, in contrast, is categorized by entrapment in old categories; by automatic behavior that precludes attending to new signals; and by action that operates from a single perspective.* (1997, p. 4.)

We believe that implementations of person-centered planning will be disappointing if people rigorously apply a procedure without sufficient regard for the context of relationships and agreements necessary for it to thrive. When such an abstraction leads people to view person-centered planning as a tool, poor results will generate efforts to sharpen or modify the tool rather than leading to a further search for new categories, the consideration of more information, and the articulation of other perspectives. Instead of building and strengthening personal relationships when difficulty comes, people fiddle with technique. In short, mindlessness about context converts person-centered planning from a useful idea into a fad.

A brief description of the way one approach to person-centered planning developed may help in remembering the features of a context in which person-centered planning makes sense.

Person-centered planning as we know it began about eighteen years ago* as a conscious search for new categories through which to understand the experience of people with developmental disabilities and work with them and their allies to change that experience for the better. This search grew, in part, out of careful study of dozens of service programs from the perspective of the principle of normalization as defined by *PASS 3* (Wolfensberger & Glenn, 1975), in part from excitement about new approaches to assisting people that put integrated school experiences, jobs, and apartment living within the reach of most if not all people with disabilities, and in part from an interest promoting different ways to facilitate effective problem solving. It was motivated by a sense of wonder at the eloquence and clarity so many people with disabilities, so many families, and so many direct service workers discovered if only someone took the time to listen carefully and imaginatively.

It was clear that old categories —which had driven institutional reform, deinstitutionalization, and the growth of local services with their focus on accurate diagnosis, therapeutic interventions, and developing skills in small steps— were insufficient to carry people into as full a life as developing technologies of assistance and instruction could support. New procedures directed attention away from questions that generated responses within old categories – questions of the type "What's wrong with you and how can professionals fix it?"– toward such questions as "What are your capacities and gifts and what supports do you need to express them?" and "What works well for you and what does not?" and "What are your visions and dreams of a brighter future and who will help you move toward that future?"

---

* We acknowledge the sustained and creative work of our friends Dottie Adams, Pat Puckett, Viola Perry, and Gillian Grable in developing the approach to person-centered planning we know best.

Person-centered planning did not ignore disability, it simply shifted the emphasis to a search for capacity in the person, among the person's friends and family, in the person's community, and among service workers. A person's difficulties were not relevant to the process until how the person wanted to live was clear. Then it was necessary to imagine, and take steps to implement, creative answers to this key question, "What particular assistance do you need because of your specific limitations (not labels) in order to pursue the life that we have envisioned together?"

This search happened at the outer edges of service systems, with people assisted by agencies that sought to offer fundamentally different sorts of service, or people whose behaviors or needs for personal assistance severely challenged existing programs, or people who fell outside available funds. It happened voluntarily; people made time to come to meetings and to work on implementation because they were interested in the person and in the process. They met in response to an invitation, not because attendance was mandatory.

It was clear to us that established procedures for individual program planning (IPP) muted the voices of people with disabilities, family and friends, and direct service workers and amplified the voices of people who occupied clinical roles. Though representatives of the different disciplines comprising a team might argue, and though there were efforts to get "input" from parents and people with disabilities, IPP's were dominated by a bureaucratic-professional perspective. Attempts to multiply perspectives led to new groundrules and procedures: we will strive to look things first and last from the person's point of view; we will look for images and words that everyone can use; personal commitment and knowledge are the basis of involvement and authority rather than professional role or administrative responsibility; meetings will happen at times and in places that are most comfortable for the person and their family; we will make time to share at least a bit of one another's lives, at least by sharing conversation about our lives, and very often by sharing food; we will try to improve our ability to include the person in decision making and to listen respectfully and imaginatively to the person's words and gestures, and to the lessons of the person's history as we construct it together.

A focus on immediate, practical action steps served to integrate different, and often conflicting, perspectives. Much of the art of facilitation lies in successfully convening people and assisting them to consider different points of view in a way that focuses more on what people can commit to do together than on what divides them. Action plans paced the need for additional meetings to check-in, problem solve, review and revise, commiserate, and celebrate. A sense of shared struggles and triumphs, however small, further strengthened relationships and commitment. Action plans often had implications for what service workers did. Sometimes these changes needed to be negotiated through the person's IPP. Sometimes these changes required changes of policy or program design. Because the process took place outside the formal structure, a commitment to work to help something happen couldn't ever be taken as a guarantee to deliver. "We will each check with people we know and meet next week to share leads to an outdoor job you can do with other men; then we'll decide what to do next." is much different than "You will have the job of your dreams by six months from Tuesday."

New information poured out. Listening and representing and taking action on the different pieces of a person's life carried by the person and those who know and care about the person, but often unshared between them, produced "ah ha" experiences for many participants. Imagining desirable futures together and then taking concrete steps toward them generated excitement and the resolve to keep looking for a way through when barriers threatened. People took joy in thinking and acting "outside the box", especially as small fragments of a person's dream began to come true.

One parent said it memorably, "All my son's life professionals have come with little boxes to fill him into. What has been different about this is that we started with a blank piece of paper and a question, 'Who is your son and what does he need to have a good future?' That has made a big positive difference, even though we haven't come close to figuring everything out yet."

People discovered that some community members were willing to join in, if the invitation were clear enough. People learned that some simple things –like changing roommates– could be beyond the reach of an agency, while some things that seemed impossible –like joining a prestigious service club– fell into place. People with disabilities and people without extended their own personal networks and sometimes themselves got help from the person they came to help. Not every plan was implemented as first written: some people discovered that their first idea didn't suit them, others that they had reached beyond what their environment could support, still others were surprised by a new possibility along the way to the goal they had set. Where there was sufficient administrative courage to create real flexibility, patterns of service shifted as increasing numbers of people found their way to inclusive classrooms, supported jobs, and supported living places. Usually, significant changes were linked to equally important organizational changes.

This exciting information spilled over into a wide network of people hungry for news about how to make good things happen for people with disabilities. Real people with disabilities, family members, community members, and service workers and managers spoke movingly about significant changes at many of the myriad conferences convened by groups interested in systems change. Their individual stories were impressively different but there was a uniform short answer to the burning question, "How did we do it? Person-centered planning!" This information sparked a growing interest in how to do person-centered planning that led some inventors to codify their procedures and devise brief workshops for training people to carry them out. As the news spread, system reformers embraced person-centered planning as part of the answer to one or more difficult questions that faced them, including, "How do we guarantee that people are better off in local services than in an institution?" and "How do we 'convert' our activity center to supported employment?" and "How do we 'tap into' natural supports for people?" and "How do we 'do' self-determination?" and even, "How do we implement managed care?" Harnessed to large scale bureaucratic reforms, demand for applying the tool has taken off. And many sensible people suggest that "the PCP" should simply replace "the IPP". After all, they reason, if this is as good a thing as it seems, it would be unfair to keep it for only a select few.

This enthusiasm is not necessarily bad news. Paying attention to people's unique capacities and listening better to what really matters to people and striving to follow through more directly on what we hear seem like reasonable disciplines to practice. There was no golden age of person-centered planning whose loss we lament and to which we want to return. For much of its history, person-centered planning directly touched only a few people, and, more often than not, service system policies and typical program designs have posed major barriers to those people's futures. If a link to person-centered planning as a tool will hasten and deepen fundamental system reforms, there is no compelling reason to be precious about it.

There is, however, reason to remember the process that generated the changes that were captured in the stories that sparked authoritative interest in widespread implementation. Absent this process –the practice of mindfulness in situations of personal engagement with people for whom change is urgent– good things may happen, but they will probably be different things from those chronicled in the more dramatic stories that many PCP trainers use to warrant their claim on people's attention. Given mindfulness, people interested in substantial change may be able to animate some aspects of almost any situation. Given, additionally, organizational commitment to spend money and offer assistance in fundamentally different ways, agencies and even systems may well break new ground.

A set of contrasts between the context in which person-centered planning developed and the context of large scale implementation may help to frame the challenges by highlighting incentives to mindlessness and opportunities for mindful work.

Person-centered planning grew as a voluntary commitment among interested people. Now it is often required for people with disabilities, their families, and staff. Mindful work involves actively inviting people to participate and encouraging participants to be clear about their personal commitment (or their inability) to take action, outside system scheduled meetings and activities, on behalf of the person's future. This commitment often begins with the facilitator accepting responsibility for her or his own personal investment in the person.

Person-centered planning grew by convening people who know and care about a person and helping them to organize. Now it may involve people with little real experience or knowledge of the person, such as the service coordinator who attended a recent conference with the question, "How do I do PCP's for the 185 people on my caseload?" Some people rely for continuity in their lives on staff who turn over very rapidly or on case mangers whose burden of paperwork leaves them little or no time to share a meal or just hang around with a person long enough to become familiar, person-to-person. Mindful work involves confronting people's isolation and seeking ways to help the person recruit allies.

Person-centered planning grew as a search for ways to integrate different perspectives into a vivid sense of a brighter future and a clear plan of action. Now some people seem to want to shrink the perspectives available to a person, sometimes by leaving family members out, sometimes by leaving service workers out, and sometimes by leaving the person alone, as if the person's solo voice were the only sound that counts. Mindful work involves helping people to discover the power in different points of view, different ideas, and different experiences in constructing an harmonious view of the future.

Person-centered planning grew with a handful of people for whom change was urgent. Now large numbers of people may be mandated to attend meetings as a matter of routine. Mindful work involves overcoming a sense of drudgery and dread at the numbers of unfinished plans and being alert to organize concerted action in situations where real change can happen.

Person-centered planning grew at the edge of the system, taking its own time, and seeking resources wherever they might be found. Now it moves toward the center. In some cases it is an instrument for implementing policies intended to comply with court mandated time tables, or ration system funds, or reduce system costs. It may fall under system regulation, for example through prescribed amounts of time for meetings, or required methods, or follow up action dictated arbitrarily rather than paced by the tempo of implementing an action plan. Mindful work involves clarity about the agendas a system has assigned and creativity in making the best of these constraints.

Person-centered planning grew as a way to increase the power held by people with disabilities; this meant creatively stepping into conflicts among family members and with service practices and policies. Now many people involved in person-centered planning complain that "parents don't support" or that "the system doesn't make it easy." Mindful work involves developing the courage to notice the potential in conflicting interests and to find ways to shift the circumstances that generate conflict to the person's advantage, no matter how slightly.

Person-centered planning grew as a way to engage people in sharing, understanding, and unfolding one another's stories. Now some people want to evaluate the effectiveness of person-centered planning by counting it's outcomes, sometimes in pre-defined categories; for them people's stories are "anecdotes". Mindful work involves remembering that people's emerging life stories are not anecdotes and that the outside evaluator's tally marks are simply one more point of view.

Person-centered planning grew as a search for new concepts, new ways to involve people with different perspectives, and new information that would lead to the creation of new community memberships for people with disabilities and new ways to support people in those memberships. It's purpose was to change community life and service practice. Now it is often done in service settings that have not embraced the need for profound change. In such settings people may complain that "We did a PCP but she still over-eats." Mindful work means avoiding the unspoken pressure to turn person-centered planning into one more way to change the person for his or her own good and finding ways to enroll people in significant changes.

It is too soon to know what will come of widespread talk about person-centered planning. It may join the hula hoop in the museum of past fads. The opportunities that come from mindful engagement in assisting people with disabilities to define and move toward desirable personal futures as community members will endure.

References

Langer, E. (1997) *The power of mindful learning.* Reading, MA: Addison Wesley.

Wolfensberger, W. & Glenn, L. (1975). *PASS 3.* Downsview, ON: National Institute on Mental Retardation.

Think Before You Plan

Michael W. Smull

Be sure to think before you plan. Thinking about a few issues before you get started can help you achieve a better outcome, prevent problems, avoid unnecessary struggle, and save you from public embarrassment. The plans being discussed here are not plans done in training, but the ordinary, day to day efforts to understand how someone wants to live and what we are going to do about it. The overriding principle is that a plan is not an outcome, the life that the person wants is the outcome. The only acceptable reason to plan is to help someone move toward the life that they desire.

Make sure that there is a commitment to act on what is learned. Remember that a plan is an organized way of learning what is important to someone and a description of what we will do to act on what have learned, including addressing any issues of health and safety.

More specifically, find out why is this plan being done with this person now? Is the purpose to…

… help the person move to a new setting

… help the person get more of what is important to them where they currently live

… to create a better understanding of how to help us support them in the life that they want while addressing issues such as a challenging behavior or a complex medical need

Once the purpose is understood, ask what you need to learn and how best to learn it. Remember, essential lifestyle planning is only one way to learn. If the person has a clear goal that will take some time to achieve think about using PATH. If the person has a number of people who care deeply, who are not exclusively paid staff, and you have the skills and energy to mobilize these relationships, think about doing a personal futures plan. Keep in mind that you can do part or all of an essential lifestyle plan to support the development or implementation of another kind of plan.

Try to learn of the challenges and issues present in developing and implementing the plan before you begin. If this is a person whose parents or guardians have views of what is important to the person that are different from the views of the person, try to determine how those differences can be addressed. It usually helps to set aside time to listen and find common ground before formal meetings. Always talk with the focus person about their options and support them in deciding how to proceed. Occasionally the best short term solution is to not to do a full plan but to help the person find the best short term compromise.

Do not forget that while someone may want something that their parents see as unsafe, they may also want to maintain a good relationship with their parents.

Do not forget that we all want mutually exclusive things (e.g. to be skinny and eat whatever we want, or to be rich and work in human services) and that part of your job is to learn what these mutually exclusive things are and to help the person find a balance that works for them.

Where what the person wants is not supported by those whose consent or assistance is needed for that person to get it, be careful. Do not engage in a process where hopes are raised, only to be crushed. Be honest about what you can do.

Remember that the best negotiation is one that no one notices. If you can learn about likely conflicts before that planning starts, you can design a process through which...

... everyone feels that they were listened to and that they participated in a respectful process

... common ground is identified and nurtured; this often starts with agreement that all of us have the same ultimate goals: that the person we are planning with to be happy and safe.

... a dialogue about a balance that will work for the person (and the compromises that will work for others) is initiated and supported.

Do not forget the most important part: spending time with the person with whom you are planning before you start the plan to get to know the person and their issues, develop the ground rules for planning, and do any negotiation necessary to have a successful outcome

Develop ground rules about who to talk with, what can and cannot be discussed, and how to keep the person informed. When the ground rules that the person wants would interfere with them getting the life they want, ground rules are negotiated before the planning starts.

Look for opportunities to build relationships and help the person be connected to their community. Look for opportunities to…

… strengthen and extend current relationships and to build new relationships

… build partnerships among those who know and care about the person and with the community

… help the person find situations where their gifts and contributions are appreciated and used.

Do not forget that an acceptable outcome from thinking before you plan is to decide not to plan. If the plan cannot be done respectfully, if there is no commitment to implement, do not plan. If the reason for planning is not acceptable do not plan. If planning is mandated, then the support and monitoring needed to insure respectful planning, and make reasonable efforts to act on what was learned must also be mandated and provided.

The Politics of Person-centered Planning

John O'Brien & Connie Lyle O'Brien

A team of regional administrators recently met an unexpected conflict with their largest service provider around a pilot project to bring self-determination to some of the people on their waiting list. With that provider's involvement and agreement, the region adopted person-centered planning as its vehicle for determining the service requirements of project participants. At the point of implementation, significant conflict arose around who would facilitate the person-centered planning process. System managers advocate that project participants choose from among a group of trained facilitators external to any service. Provider managers oppose this, arguing that their staff are experienced and capable in the techniques of person-centered planning and that participants' choice should not be limited arbitrarily, especially since a number of parents of people on the waiting list had already expressed interest in the provider's services. Because the provider agency has a strong constituency built on its tradition of local service, system managers lack the power to control the issue despite their formal authority as service purchasers. Because system managers notice that all of the provider's person-centered plans call for one or another of the services the agency already provides, most of which are typical congregate programs, they are unwilling to assign the provider responsibility for defining self-determination by implementing the process. Desiring to rise above the conflict, system managers requested assistance in locating an objectively validated standard for defining person-centered planning which would prove the necessity of independent facilitation.

To read this situation simply, as an example of the sort of conflict of interest that justifies external service coordination, would miss important lessons about the limits of person-centered planning. The most basic lesson is this. Person-centered planning belongs to the politics of community and disability. It is not a way to avoid conflict about the investment of public resources; it is one way to creatively seek principled resolutions of real and enduring conflicts in collaboration with people with disabilities who want to consider a change in their lives that requires organized support from other people or adaptation of available service practices or policies.

Person-centered planning offers a forum for dealing with contested questions in the lives of particular people and in the histories of particular organizations, communities, and states. These conflicts not only concern public policy, they are also integral to the politics of everyday life. Put generally, these related, conflicted questions include:

- What social roles and opportunities for economic and civic participation will be open to people with disabilities? When will people participate as clients of a disability service and when will they participate in ordinary activities and places, with accommodation and support?
- How will the work of adapting to and assisting people with disabilities be divided among…
  … family members (including extended family)
  … community associations (such as churches and civic clubs)
  … public services and amenities (such as schools and hospitals, and transit systems and parks)
  … actors in the marketplace (such as landlords, employers, co-workers, bankers, and dentists)
  … specialized disability services
- How will existing investments and practices be regarded when they become inconsistent with changing appreciation of the rights of people with disabilities and rapidly evolving technologies for assistance?

These political questions tend to hide in the background of person-centered planning efforts. Often they hide behind two principles of practice: "We are making change one person at a time" and "We listen to the person and honor the person's choices." These slogans describe the discipline of person-centered planning and are good and helpful as far as they go. They become unhelpful when they obscure the powerful effects that personal and organizational positions on political questions have on the process of person-centered planning.

Focusing on one person at a time makes it possible to diversify opportunities by following different individual interests into distinct sectors of community life and allows learning about how to personalize the assistance required to fit individual circumstances. However, it can become an excuse for avoiding the administrative work necessary to make service system resources flexible and responsive to individual differences. Low organizational capacity to learn from the ways in which person-centered planning increases uncertainty and anxiety creates the meaning of "one person at a time" depicted in the diagram below: the number of people engaged, and the depth of listening for developmental change will be paced by the level of anxiety the organization can already tolerate.

One person at a time…

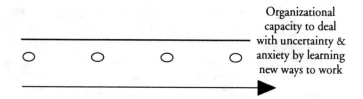

An organization can choose to use person-centered planning as a dis-organizer to stimulate learning when its members commit themselves to deal constructively with the anxiety generated by discovering that people's aspirations and needs could be better served than current practice, program design, and policy allows. A growing capacity to learn allows engagement with more people whose diverse requests direct and pace development, as depicted below.

One person at a time…

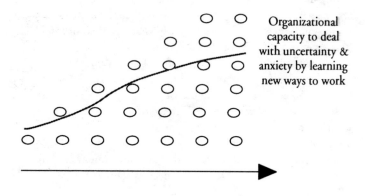

Listening is an engaged process, not a matter of impersonally recording answers to questions like "What matters most in the way you live?" One's stand on political issues inevitably governs one's listening and problem solving. Listeners committed to shaping local workplaces to adapt to the needs of workers with disabilities will hear people's desire to find a job; listeners committed to providing a sheltered alternative to workplace demands will hear people's desire for improvements within congregate environments. Problem-solvers who believe that services exist to take the burden of care off as many families and community settings as funds allow will recognize and organize very different resources than problem-solvers who see family and community members as making an irreplaceable contribution to people's quality of life. Listeners from organizations committed to going out of the business of providing group living in favor of supporting people's lives in their own homes will hear that more people want their own places; listeners from organizations that want to offer a range of group and semi-independent alternatives will hear more desire for transfers within that range of settings.

The interactive nature of listening makes the politics of community and disability inescapable, and consciousness of the effects of one's own positions essential. Indeed, reflection on what possibilities people choose to explore in one's presence can sharpen consciousness of the position one lives in. If most all the people one plans with seem pretty happy in their group homes, this suggests a definite position on the roles and opportunities that should be available to people with disabilities.

When a listener who believes that people with disabilities belong in typical workplaces meets a person who believes that they or their family member are well served in a sheltered setting, a political issue appropriately enters the process. This conflict can energize inquiry, understanding, and creative action on whatever areas of agreement may emerge, but only if the existence of the conflict and its stakes are openly acknowledged and explored. There is no excuse for dishonoring people by leaving this conflict unspoken, though it can best find voice in respectful and civil tones. There is no objective position above the issue from which to listen, though the disciplines of suspending automatic reactions to difference, balancing inquiry about other's perceptions and beliefs with advocacy for one's own, and searching for possibilities for shared commitment are fundamental to creating the shared space necessary for effective work.

We think it good practice to orient the person-centered planning process by making clear what resources are on the table as people begin. A simple framework can help clarify the space in which person-centered planning happens by noting the limitations on the process. **Social resources** include family members committed to their understanding of the person's well being, allies and friends who have chosen to make the person part of their own lives, memberships the person can claim, networks of contacts, information, and influence available to the person and those around the person, and the person's consequent wealth. Social resources can be more or less extensive, more or less diverse, and more or less aligned and organized for action. **Service resources** include available public funds, the capacity of service agencies to personalize assistance to people in community settings, and the interest of agencies and their staff in learning new ways to work and organize themselves in partnership with the people they plan with. Service resources can be more or less sufficient to the task, more or less flexible, and exhibit higher or lower levels of commitment and urgency. Service resources can be

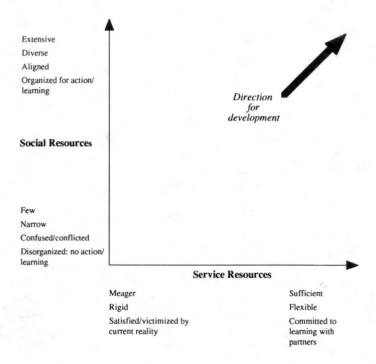

more or less sufficient to the task, more or less flexible, and exhibit higher or lower levels of commitment and urgency.

Person-centered planning will be weak when there is no explicit, creative, and sustained effort to increase both social resources, by supporting the person to recruit new people and try new roles, and service resources, by challenging agency and system to higher levels of personalization and flexibility. Of course, social prejudice and agency or system inertia can defeat such efforts. The reason for person-centered planning is to assure that more and more people encourage one another to try for significant change and sustain one another to keep on working despite defeat.

People who are working for real change will find themselves in the midst of political conflict. Their civic action will produce the single most reliable indicator that person-centered planning is really happening in a service system: agency and system administrators will find themselves sweating as they deal with the uncertainties and anxieties and conflicts of fitting their organizational efforts better to the lives of the people they serve.

6

Revisiting Choice

Michael W. Smull

Choice is the most powerful word and the most abused word in the current lexicon of the disabilities services system. For some people choice means that how they want to live has been discovered and carefully supported. For others choice is an excuse or the basis of a bizarre rationalization. Perhaps because choice is the word de jour, it has been used to argue that congregate facilities are needed in order to ensure residential "choice". An even more egregious example is justifying the use of pain to control behavior to allow "choice among a full range of treatment options". (The same argument could be made to retain "bleeding" as a treatment option for the flu.) Other abuses are more subtle. When you look behind the rhetoric of agencies which say "we offer and teach choice", you find places that ask people what they want to wear but not who they want to live with. What appears to be absent is depth of under-standing and a sense of balance. A single word is being used for complex concepts. Too often, there is no recognition of the need for an individual balance between honoring choice and ensuring safety.

Preferences, opportunities, and control

Choice, as it is being used in current disability discussions, appears to have three related concepts embedded in it –preferences, oppor-tunities, and control.

Preferences include not only what someone likes but also their desires and dreams. Preferences include: who people want to spend time with; what to do during that time; and where to spend their time.

Opportunities are the available array of: people to spend time with; things to do during that time; and places to spend that time. Opportunities should also include being able to spend time by yourself. Preferences reflect what people want while opportunities reflect what is available.

Control is the authority to make use of an opportunity to satisfy a preference.

Looking at preferences, desires, and dreams

Any effort to support choice should start with discovering what is important to the people who are being supported. What do people want in their relationships with others? How do people want to spend their time? What do people want to do (and not do)? What kinds of environments in general and what specific places do people want to spend time in or avoid? Do people have dreams about how they would like to live and do they have nightmares about what they are afraid will happen to them? While answers to these questions are sought (with varying degrees of emphasis) in all of the formal processes for person-centered planning, careful efforts are required.

Many people lack the life experiences necessary to know what they like and dislike. Will something that sounds desirable to a person feel that way when it is experienced? Some people want to try things or live in ways that put their safety or health (or both) at risk Many people need to have a life of their own before they can have a dream of their own. As people try things (and as they age) their preferences change. In a system that offers real choice, people continuously have opportunities and are continuously supported in expressing their preferences. Supporting choice requires that there be recognition that everyone has preferences and desires regardless of the severity of disability. Supporting choice also requires that we recognize that what we need to know is taught by the people that we support. Some of what my colleagues and I have learned about preferences from the people that we have listened to follows.

We have taught learned helplessness, now we need to teach trust. Many people have experienced systematic ignoring of their preferences. This is an unintended consequence of current "individual" planning and professional practice within the disability system. We cope with the poverty of opportunities for the people we support by suppressing their preferences for what is absent. "Learned helplessness" has been taught and many of those we support have learned this lesson well. For these people, what needs to be taught is that we can be trusted.

Trust is "taught" by having those with control listen to all expressions of preference and, where possible (and sensible), to help people get what they want. "Teaching choice" is a poor label. Those who teach must remember that they are not "offering choices" but soliciting preferences and then demonstrating that staff can be trusted to honor the preference expressed. Staff must learn to acknowledge the preferences that people are expressing with their behavior while not asking what people want until there is a commitment to honor their requests.

Shouting (with behavior) has sometimes been the only way to be heard. Most of us have had the experience of raising our voices in the belief that it will increase understanding. We shout so that we will be heard. A number of people with disabilities have learned to "shout" with their behavior because it is the only way that they are heard. If you do not like your current job, complaining about it does not produce change. Acting in unacceptable ways does produce change. Complaining about who you live with is unlikely to get you a new roommate, but aggression often works. "Shouting" gets our attention, but rarely gets people what they really want. We need to listen for the preference that is underneath the shouting. Once real preferences are understood (and acted on), the need for "shouting" with behavior is eliminated (although the person may always be someone who has a loud "voice").

Most of what people want is modest

What people want is usually modest. When critics say that we cannot afford choice they have typically confounded what is important to people with what might be nice to have. There is also a difference between learning what is important to people and taking someone on a guided fantasy. Careful planning discovers preferences such as: having a say in who helps me; having privacy in the bathroom; being asked not ordered; going for a walk when I want; and (for one person who uses a wheelchair) to be able to control the direction in which I face.

A few people's desires are not modest. While the vast majority of people have modest desires, there are a few people who sincerely want frequent trips to the tropics, a car continuously at their disposal, and support staff who take on the role of servants. They may see these as essential to a reasonable quality of life. They are "virtual yuppies", without the income needed to support their desired lifestyle. They are also unusual, as careful planning identifies very few people with these expensive tastes. Where rational decisions are being made about allocation of resources, these people are disappointed with the outcome.

Some people have reasonable requests that are difficult to afford. The fact that someone wants something, even if they see it as very important, does not mean that it has to be delivered. However, we do have an obligation to respond to sincere requests as we can. For example, there are many people who would like to try living by themselves. The cost of support (in staff and housing) presents a real challenge to those attempting to create a system of support. The demand for living alone is somewhat reduced when there is more careful listening. For example, some people really do not want to live alone but simply do not want to live with other people with disability labels. Other people have always had to share lives (e.g. it is Tuesday so we all go bowling) and have not learned that you can also live with someone where you only share space.

After these situations have been clarified there are still many people who simply want to have the experience of living by themselves. Where people have been able to live by themselves for a year or two, many would like to have a roommate for company (but not to share lives with). Some people, however, find that living alone is the only way they wish to live. The support costs for most of these people decline dramatically as behaviors change, skills are learned, and connections to the community are built. However, the cost of support for some people remains high. From the perspective of a system, a small percentage of people can always be supported in relatively expensive lives. The challenge is to not have that percentage exceed the resources available.

What people don't want is as important as what they do want. In learning people's preferences, it is important to discover what they dislike. Simple lists are not adequate; we must go beyond a statement that George likes barbecues and dislikes broccoli. We have a significant degree of control over who we spend time with and what we do. We use that control to avoid people and activities that we strongly dislike. People with disabilities have not had that control. In the absence of being able to "vote with your feet" we need to insure that those things that people hate or strongly dislike are absent.

Choice making is not a solitary activity

Figuring out what we want is usually not a solitary activity. To tell people that yesterday we made the choices and that today they are in charge is to ignore that few of us make significant choices without discussion. Before we make major decisions, such as changing jobs or changing partners, we have typically discussed the "pros and cons" at some length. We seek advice, support, and people who just listen. We strive to determine what is right for us. We frequently get conflicting advice and pick the advice that agrees with what we want. We reserve the right to make "bad" choices after we have heard the "good" advice. People with disabilities need the same opportunities.

What people ask for may not be what they want. People will ask for those things that they know about. One woman who was being assisted in leaving an institution said that she wanted to move to a "group home". One man said that he wanted to live alone. The woman who said that she wanted to live in a group home spoke very little English. She knew that she wanted to leave the institution and the only place away from the institution that she knew of was a "group home". The man who said he wanted to live by himself thought that the only choices that existed were to live by himself or with other people with disabilities. The woman is living happily in supported living and the man is living in a house that he wanted where he rents rooms to five people who have no formal disability labels.

When people express a desire for a job (or anything else) where their disability or circumstances preclude obtaining what is asked for, we need to listen to what lies beneath the surface. One man said he wanted to be a pilot. After a lot of discussion we discovered that while he did want to be a pilot he also just loved airplanes. We could not help him become a pilot but we could help him get a job at an airport.

Some years ago I worked with another man who said that he wanted to have a job just like his father's. His father is a well known research scientist with the federal government who determined what projects got funded. Many conversations later we found that the characteristics that mattered to him were that he be treated with the same respect that his father received and that he wear a tie to work. We helped him find a job where he wore a tie and ran a large copying machine at a facility that did scientific research. If you were a scientist who wanted your latest journal article copied you went to his copy center. If you just filled out the form your article would get copied in turn, if you treated him with "respect" he would do your copying while you waited.

Sometimes what people want is not possible

A woman I met in the Midwest, Susie, wants to live with her mother. It is so important to her that she sees it as the only acceptable place for her to live. Unfortunately this is not possible. Susie had lived with her mother for several decades and mother had been the person who provided care and support. After a sudden loss of capacity Susie left her home and entered a hospital and then a nursing home. The supports necessary to support Susie in her mother's house are available and affordable. However, Susie's mother would not agree to her return regardless of the supports that could be provided. This is not to disparage Susie's mother. She continues to be deeply caring and intimately involved in Susie's support, but she is "burnt out" as a caregiver.

In these circumstances our obligation is to acknowledge and honor the positions of both Susie and her mother. Honoring her mother's position requires that we not use guilt or otherwise coerce her to support Susie's return to her home. It requires that we support her in developing her new relationship with her daughter. Honoring Susie's position requires that we acknowledge what is important to her and help her get on with her life. We have to avoid the temptation to deny the presence of a preference that cannot be realized. We also have to help Susie deal with a very real loss and to help her begin to develop new relationships. She needs support in her changing relationship with her mother and in developing new relationships.

Helping people be safe and happy requires thought and effort

One of the traps of the current system of planning is that we determine how people can be safe before we look at what they require to be happy. We forget that there is no such thing as a risk free life, that risk is relative and has a context. What we need is to begin with an understanding of what is required for the "pursuit of happiness" and then seek to reduce or avoid risk within that context. What is not acceptable is to simply say it was his choice, that is why I stood by while he hurt himself. Helping people be happy and safe requires thought and creativity. The following stories give some examples of the efforts needed.

A story that I enjoy telling (and writing about) is that of a man who wants to go for walks whenever he wants and who also thinks that, when he crosses a street, traffic should stop for him. The initial thinking was that he needed one-to-one staffing across all waking hours. The cost of the staffing necessary for a couple of walks each day was an expense that was disproportionate to the result. On the other hand not being able to go for walks on his schedule significantly reduced the quality of his life. Further discussion lead us to realize that this man would be happy to live in a rural setting. He moved to a house on a five acre Christmas tree farm where he goes for walks whenever he wants without having to cross a street.

One man that we did planning with liked to use "found objects" in his art projects. The challenge was that he would "find" objects in stores and leave without paying for them. He understood the concept of money but was remarkably uninterested in it. The people who supported him could have said that it was his "choice" and let him be arrested. Instead they would go to stores with him, with his money in their pocket. (He would give his money away if it was in his pocket.) As they left each store the support staff would ask if he had "found" something in that store and, if yes, the staff would pay for it.

We got a phone call several years ago from a service provider asking for help with someone who was severely injuring himself. This man is now described as a tall, charming, ladies man who does not use words to talk. At the time, his brother said that he looked like a hockey goalie with the helmet and all of the padding that he wore to keep from injuring himself. There were people who said that he needed a "more restrictive" setting and there were people who said that pain should be used to control his behavior. The service provider could have argued that an institution would be the "safe place" for him to be. Instead we were asked to help the provider "listen" to what this man was asking for.

After listening to what he was saying with his behavior and after listening to what those who loved him knew, we found that there was no single answer. However, there were a host of simple things that we could do. There were many ways in which we were not listening to how he wanted to live. Some examples include that he: needs to close all doors (except for his bedroom door at night) and to line up all shoes; must be able to make and eat his own snacks when he wants them (including raw onions with salt); must not be ignored (even if it is planned); and he must always have a non-glossy magazine to hold onto. His life is not perfect and he still gets upset occasionally. On these infrequent occasions he still needs people who keep him from hurting himself. However, because we have been listening carefully to what he is asking for he is living in his community. He lives (and goes to concerts with his brother) without pads, splints, or a helmet.

Choice requires opportunities and sharing control

A preference is something that people want. Unless they have already experienced it they will not know whether they like it or not. Many people with disabilities have never had the life experiences necessary to determine how they really want to live. Honoring choice for these people requires opportunities and taking advantage of the opportunities may require encouragement. As people begin to find that their choices are honored, they want control over those choices. Honoring choice requires that control is shared.

Choice, as we are using it, is a simple word that contains three concepts –preferences opportunities, and control. Learning people's preferences is a complex and on-going activity. What people want, and the values that underlie their desires, provides a picture of how people want to live. However, learning how people want to live is only the beginning. It is the necessary foundation but just the foundation. In order to get the life that you want and to maintain it. you need opportunities and control.

For people with disabilities the absence of control and opportunities is a devastating combination. Flooding people with opportunities or simply handing over control can be equally devastating. Everyone needs opportunities and everyone needs control but they need them on their own terms. People who have never had opportunities need to sample life in their own way. Some people need to dive in. They do not want and cannot tolerate transitions. Others are most comfortable with first putting a toe in. They want lengthy and careful transitions. Both need the control necessary to change their minds. Some people have been demanding control over significant aspects of their lives, and we have seen them as having challenging behaviors. Some have given up hope, and we see them as withdrawn or even as compliant. However, regardless of the severity of disability, people want control over parts of their lives.

Providing opportunities, sharing control

Having control is how we maintain a balance in our own lives. Each of us needs control sufficient to keep (or secure) what we value in our lives and to reject (or leave) situations that we cannot stand.

One definition of emotional health is that we recognize what a balance is and that we recognize opportunities that enable us to maintain or enhance that balance. That is, we are able to use opportunities to get more of what we value or less of what we dislike. Control is what allows us to try new things and discard them when they do not fit. Control is what we require when we find our lives out of balance, and we look for the opportunities that will bring a positive balance. The situations we find the most frustrating are those where we lack control, and/or where the opportunities that we need are absent.

Control is a complex concept

Having control means that we have to make decisions, and all of us create a set of positive rituals or routines that allow us to get through much of our day without treating each situation as if it were new. Most of us do not want absolute control. We may joke that if were in charge of the world we could fix things, but most of us want (and welcome) limits to the areas where we have to make decisions. We conform to large sets of societal rules without much thought and only remark on those few areas where we disagree. Those of us who live with others find that we have to share control. Each of us has our own rules that we insist that our partner honor and our partners expect the same of us. Where expectations regarding behavior are not met, or are mutually exclusive, conflict arises. The outcome of a resolved conflict is a mutual agreement on the behaviors expected. Our vision of the best outcome is that our partners will see the error of their ways and the wisdom of our words. A more rational outcome is that each of us will better understand the other and make the compromise that works for the relationship. In reciprocal relationships control is shared.

If we apply what works for everyone to people with disabilities, then we should be helping people with disabilities to have sufficient control to maintain a balance in their lives and to create their own rituals and routines. We should help them develop relationships (both paid and unpaid) where control is shared. A brief description of what the disability system should be doing is: to discover how people want to live; provide them with the opportunities necessary to get the lives they want; and help them have the control needed to maintain it. Many of the challenges in doing this arise from the disabling environments in which people have lived. We have created these environments with a binary view of control. Either I have control, or you have control. The idea that control can and should be shared seems to be an alien concept.

Control, opportunities, and preferences as developmental triplets

Parents support the development of their children by asking the child to choose from alternatives and then honoring the choice the child makes. As children grow in capacity and experience the span of control gets broader. Children may move from what they will wear, to when they will go to bed, to how they spend most of their waking hours. They move from nearly constant supervision to doing what they want within defined (and often disputed) boundaries. Parents transfer control slowly. All parents worry about whether their children are "ready". When a child breaks a rule about the boundaries of behavior, the child loses control for a time (smaller children may go to their rooms, older children may be "grounded"). Parents share control with their children while they are transferring it. Typical children go through phases where they rely on their parents control for most things, go through a period were they both want and do not want parental control (teenagers can simultaneously tell their parents that they are ruining their lives while wanting limits to push against), and end up, as adults, with control regardless of their parents desires.

For people with disabilities the analogy with the developmental process that children pass through is both helpful and dangerous. It is helpful in that it provides some guidance as to where someone is and how we might help them move forward in a safe and rational way. The analogy breaks down as the inevitability of autonomy for typical children is not present for people with disabilities. It is dangerous in that we are talking of supporting adults who may have already been trapped by developmental concepts such as mental age.

Control and capacity

How much control we have, and what we have control over, should be a function of desire and capacity. However, our stereotypes of people with severe cognitive impairments cause us to over look the capacities that are present. I have met a number of people who do not use words to talk but who are good at training staff in listening to their behaviors with regard to what they want. They demonstrate a much greater capacity for (and interest in)controlling their lives than they are given credit for. At the same time we need to recognize that positive control is learned, and control should be coupled with a knowledge of consequences.

We need to ask what are people asking for and how can we help them get it without putting them at unnecessary risk. It can be as simple as supporting Rhonda, who uses a wheel chair, in being where she wants to be. Any sunny warm day she will want to go outside and enjoy the sun. Unfortunately she is also very allergic to pollen and needs to be told, on days with a high pollen count, that she would not enjoy the consequences of going outside.

Timing and opportunities

Timing is important in how people respond to opportunities. We tell our friends that we are not ready or that we will do it when we are ready. Opportunities have a developmental sequence, people need to be offered what they are ready to try. What people are ready for and when they will be ready requires judgment. Given the uneven, but generally impoverished, life experiences that people have had they need to be encouraged to try new things. They may need to have an opportunity presented again and again. Judgment is required to determine where encouragement stops and coercion starts. At the same time a lack of experience coupled with uneven deficits in skills and capacities makes people more vulnerable. Opportunities can lead to injury and judgment is again required. There is little growth that comes without risk. People need to be able to fail and to feel hurt. Supporting people in having opportunities so that we will know what they will want tomorrow is as important as it is to learn what people want now.

What opportunities we provide, hold back, encourage people to find, or protect people from depends as much on our values as they do on the preferences and capacities of the people we support. We need to listen to ourselves when we say that someone is not ready or that they should be able to do something simply because it is their choice. Our values influence and often control what we support. We need to talk about what our values are so that we understand the basis on which we are making decisions. We need to remember that the opportunities that are made available depend on the values of those with control.

Looking for control

Most of us seek, and to a large degree achieve, the amount and kind of control that we want over major aspects of our lives. Control is part of what gives us the predictability that we value. One of the more devastating feelings that people report is being out of control or experiencing a loss of control. When we have less control than we desire, increased emphasis is placed on the control that remains. For people with disabilities who live in very controlled settings, control is sought where ever it can be found. Some of the behaviors that we want to change around food, aggression, self-injury, and sexuality are a reflection of a lack of desired control over other aspects of life. When people gain positive control over their lives the behaviors that have caused us concern may diminish, and with some people vanish.

There is an important difference between sharing control and giving control. Control is not a fixed quantity. It ebbs and flows in our relationships, and it can ebb and flow with the people we support. An agency in North Carolina that is supporting people with severe and persistent mental illnesses as well as cognitive impairments sees control as moving toward the person supported whenever possible but also returning to staff when the person supported has an acute episode. Someone with a severe seizure disorder may be able to do some things when the seizures are under control and should not have the same opportunities when the seizures are not under control.

Rethinking choice

Our recent history is filled with stories of people whose lives were totally controlled who now live in happy interdependence. People who were seen as not competent to select what to wear are now living in their own homes. We are also hearing of the people who have been injured when some one used choice as an excuse to not think. We need to recognize that the people we support are the experts on what they want while we are their partners in helping them get it. We need to have relationships where we share control and continuously support people in gaining as much control as is possible. Many people, especially those with severe disabilitie,s are only asking for modest control. They want to be able to: control the pace of life (to not be rushed); to be listened to (to only go to bed when they are sleepy); and to have a say in who their staff are (to only be supported by people that they trust).

In our relationships we should help people grow and remember that there is a dignity to risk. At the same time there is no dignity in serious injury. We need to see the key to growth as starting with understanding what people want today and then helping people find opportunities so that they will know what they want tomorrow. We need to recognize that everyone wants and needs control over some aspects of their lives. Our jobs include supporting people in gaining that control.

7

Positive Rituals and Quality of Life

Michael W. Smull

Rituals ease us through our day

Every morning when you arrive at work, you head for that first cup of coffee. Only after the cup is in your hand and you have chatted about the prior evenings events with your co-workers do you feel that you are really at work and ready to start. If there is an urgent phone call before you have that first cup of coffee in your hand, you grumble to yourself because you are not really in the office until you have your coffee. When you arrive home from work you do not feel like you are home until you have changed out of your "work clothes." Both of these are examples of the daily rituals that we employ to help us cope with transitions.

We give our daily rituals and habits scant conscious attention as they ease us through our days. Perhaps it is the absence of conscious attention that has lead us to neglect the role of ritual in the quality of life of people with disabilities. However, rituals are as much a part of quality of life for people with disabilities as they are for everyone else. Families know this. They have looked for substitutes for acquisition of the driver's license, realizing that this is the American secular rite of passage to adult life. They worked to make confirmation, bar mitzvah, and graduation ceremonies accessible to their sons and daughters. It is time for those of us who support people with disabilities to consciously consider the role of ritual and to insure the presence of positive rituals.

Daily rituals

Rituals begin every day with our morning routines. Each has a pattern of waking up and getting ready to face the day. These dally rituals are comforting. An example is bathing. Each of us has a pattern in how we wash our bodies. Is your face washed first or last? For those people who need assistance in bathing and cannot speak for themselves, the pattern of bathing may change with every change in staff. Yet when one mother in Ontario requested that her daughter's face be washed last, this was seen as an example of her being overly involved and controlling. John, who was learning how to do Essential Lifestyle Planning, was sharing the person-centered plan done on himself. He noted that he gets up slowly in the morning and does not want bright lights, loud music, or perky people around him until he has had his first cup of coffee. He described his fiancé as one of those perky morning people who bounce out of bed ready to go at full speed. Their accommodation is that she leaves the bedroom and is perky elsewhere. Because they respect and love each other, their incompatible morning rituals are accomplished without intruding on each other. Supporting the daily coping rituals of people with disabilities begins with paying attention to the personalities of those we support. Many direct care staff can tell you how they already do this, but the absence of sanction from professionals means that rituals that are supported today may be seen as non-compliant behavior tomorrow.

Maintaining and building rituals

In *Rituals for our times*, Imber-Black and Roberts (1992) describe the importance and nature of rituals for all of us. They note that: "Daily rituals define the boundary between the family and the outside world." They include all of the important minutia of our lives at home. Common rituals around food include: the times at which we eat, what food is served on special occasions; where does each person sit at the table; and do we watch TV while we eat. These reflect our current preferences and our histories. Every time new people come into a home we need to remember that they bring their preferences and history with them. In houses owned or rented by the service provider, the rituals are often those of the service provider and change as staff turn over. Where people have spent decades in institutions they may not have any rituals that work in small settings. People with disabilities and staff who come from families rich in positive rituals can help to create new rituals in the homes in which they live. However, systematic efforts to discover, build, and sustain these rituals is required.

Our efforts need to begin with these daily rituals. We have found that some of the people referred to us because of "non-compliant" or aggressive behavior simply have daily rituals that were not recognized. Our obsessions implementing program plans and continuous training have resulted in our ignoring, suppressing, and trying to replace rituals that are positive, individual adaptations to the rhythms of daily life. Once the issues are seen in this context, staff were able to accommodate the positive rituals of the individual within program schedule requirements and offer training as it made sense. Beyond the daily rituals there are others that also deserve our attention. The topography that Imber-Black and Roberts use divides rituals into those that express "relating, changing, healing, believing, and celebrating ." (p. 56) To consider the significance of these we need only look to the importance of Sundays in our own patterns of rituals. For some of us Sundays are days of spiritual renewal and relating to those who share our faith. For others of us Sunday is the day when you not only sleep late, you pad around in sleeping garb well into the afternoon. During football season, Sundays are the day when family and friends gather to yell at the television set. The Sunday rituals of each home should be the rituals of the people who live there and not be subjected to the vagaries of changing staff.

Rituals of comfort

We also need to remember that some rituals are rituals of comfort. We have sets of behaviors that we use to help us feel better when the "slings and arrows of outrageous fortune" strike us. After a bad day at work, we will go home and say to our partner "I do not want to do the chores planned for this evening. I had a really bad day at work. Let's go out for dinner or the movies instead." We say it even when it was our behavior that resulted in the bad day at work. If you are someone with a disability who goes to a day program it is not unknown to have your day program counselor call your residential counselor and say: "he was really bad at his day program, do not let him have any privileges at home tonight." We need to ask ourselves why there is a saying among self-advocates that says "Never tell them what you like because they will make you earn it. Never tell them what you dislike because they will do it to you when you are bad."

Rituals and relationship

As we look at supporting people in their communities we need to remember that much of the richness of "community" comes from the relationships that we have and the rituals that celebrate and build those relationships. Despite its central function, the role of ritual is rarely discussed. In our rapidly changing, mobile, and fragmented society, positive rituals deserve attention for all of us regardless of the presence of disabilities. For people who need substantial support to get through life, developing positive rituals should be a priority. For many people with disabilities, these rituals will need to be developed with the assistance of the staff and then supported by the staff. Once established, however, they should change at a pace dictated by the individual, not by the rate at which new staff arrive. The rituals must be rooted in who each individual is as well as each person's current circumstances. Properly used, rituals will help people through major life changes as well as daily existence. In the support plans of the future more space should be spent on how to support people in their positive rituals and less on how to program every waking moment of their lives.

Reference

Imber-Black, E. & Roberts, J. (1992). *Rituals for our times: celebrating, healing, and changing our lives and our relationships.* New York: Harper Collins.

8

More Than a Meeting

Benefits and Limitations of Personal Futures Planning

Beth Mount

Personal futures planning is an approach for learning about people with disabilities and creating a lifestyle that can help people contribute in community life. Personal futures planning is much more than a meeting; it is an ongoing process of social change. The effectiveness of a plan depends on a support group of concerned people who make a dream reality by learning to solve problems, build community, and change organizations together over time. The locus of change is moved away from the person with a disability toward change in social roles, responses, and existing organizational structures. As an ongoing process of innovation, it can help liberate people from oppressive environments and processes that are harmful.

Personal futures planning can be a helpful tool when it is used selectively to support long-range change in organizational cultures, and it can facilitate immediate changes in the quality of life experiences available to people. However, it can easily become another empty ritual if used as a quick fix without appreciation for the complex tasks of changing environments, enhancing respect and decision-making, and creating a context for friendships.

An overview of the basic assumptions and benefits of the personal futures planning approach is followed by a discussion of the breakdowns that begin when personal futures planning is implemented in a system-centered, rather than person-centered way. Finally, an effective development project is outlined to provide a hopeful alternative to methods of implementation that fail.

The way of describing people, thinking about their future, and solving problems together are among the many ways of expressing values, assumptions, and ideals. Personal futures planning is a way of planning together with people to express and live according to the values of contribution, community inclusion, and choice. This form of planning is a powerful tool because it provides the capacity to develop new visions for people, reimagine what is possible for them, and reevaluate their own roles and investments in making these ideals livable.

In contrast, traditional forms of planning are based on the ideal of a developmental model, which negates this promise of renewal by emphasizing the deficits and needs of people, overwhelming people with endless program goals and objectives, and assigning responsibility for decision-making to professionals. Traditional planning often reinforces the status quo of organizations by focusing solely on accomplishments that are possible within existing programs and structures.

The underlying values of traditional planning communicate subtle messages, for example: The person is the problem and should be fixed but never will be. Learning to adapt to impossible situations is expected; the more a person protests, the more of a problem he or she is. Professionals know best, and the person must stay in segregated programs until he or she is ready for community. These messages undermine people's confidence and growth.

Many of the positive outcomes intended by well-meaning planners are sabotaged by these messages, the bias of others more interested in the control and maintenance of people under the rubric of care is strengthened. The message to people with disabilities and their families is that the planning process is to be used to clarify their needs and deficits, to identify how they need to change to fit existing programs, and to give professionals the opportunity to feel certain that they know what is best.

Another way of thinking

Personal futures planning reflects an alternative set of values and messages. It is based on the promise of community inclusion for everyone. The logic of personal futures planning amplifies the message that people with disabilities have important gifts and capacities that seek expression. Professionals need to learn to listen to, and take direction from, individuals and families. Many of the activities, people, and experiences they enjoy provide professionals with clues to their interests that professionals hope to expand and increase. Similarly, often when situations frustrate people it means that the setting, environment, activity, or people in the situation need to change.

Personal futures planning helps the professional to change from the superior role of expert to a more humble role as a partner whose motto is: Work so that people have many ways to be a part of community life. It is our job to work to negotiate needed organizational changes to remove barriers that may stand in the way. Caring, supportive friendships are central to well-being and professionals must work with individuals and families to learn how to develop community and friendships. The contrast between the focus of traditional program plans, and the alternative vision of positive futures plans is summarized in this table (Mount, 1991b).

Characteristics of traditional program plans	Characteristics of personal futures planning
Goals focus on *decreasing* specific negative behaviors.	Images of the future anticipate that positive change will occur & affirmative activities & experiences will *increase*.
Program categories & service options that are often *segregated* are identified.	Ideas & possibilities reflect specific *community* sites & settings & valued roles in those settings.
Many goals & objectives reflect potentially *minor accomplishments* that can be attained in existing programs without making any changes.	Some ideas will seem outlandish, unrealistic, & impractical & require *major changes* in existing patterns.

The benefits of personal futures planning

Personal futures planning is most effective when it is used in conjunction with a number of other activities to question service practices and provide direction for innovation. Following are descriptions of five potential benefits of personal futures planning. Futures planning shares these benefits with planning approaches that have similar assumptions and ideals (Brost & Johnson, 1982; Forest & Snow, 1987; Green, 1984; O'Brien, 1987).

1. *A positive view of people* in personal futures planning helps professionals come to know people with disabilities and appreciate their capacities. This is a discovery process because the gifts, interests, and capacities of people with disabilities so often are buried under labels, poor reputations, and fragmentation of information. The personal profile process helps professionals see these individuals in a new light, by emphasizing their hidden

gifts. The focus on capacity as a major aspect of futures planning is powerful because it can be liberating from the institutionalized process of detached criticism built into traditional diagnosis and assessment. In my experience, once this freedom is experienced, people with disabilities, their family members, and human service workers are eager to cast off the old descriptions that limit people and discover new ways to see people. The development of a positive view often generates constructive energy and action.

2. *Motivation through inspiration* is the aspect of futures planning that develops the capacity to work for change on the basis of a common vision that feels more worthy than conventional practices. Often people feel drawn toward change when they create, invent, envision, and imagine a better life rich with community life and relationships. This motivation process offers a constructive alternative to the often boring and insulting process of traditional planning directed by endless lists of goals and objectives that lead nowhere.

3. *Personal empowerment* for people with disabilities, their families, and their friends is a goal of personal futures planning. An effective planning process can strengthen the voice and desires of the focus person in a way that enables others to respond. An effective planning process also includes people with disabilities in an ongoing process of problem-solving with the help of family and friends, thereby decreasing the control of paid professionals and, hopefully, increasing interdependence with informal support systems. When people have difficulty representing their own interests, the process seeks to inform and support those people who are most involved on a daily basis.

4. *Community involvement and development* are central to the personal futures planning process. An effective planning process seeks to widen, deepen, and strengthen relationships and community life. The community-building focus of futures planning helps redirect attention, time, energy, and resources from building systems to building personal relationships.

5. *Organizational change* is an integral part of personal futures planning. Almost every personal futures plan that is true to the person challenges the existing organizational process and structure in some way. The personal futures planning process can illuminate the shortcomings of existing organizations and lead to clear, constructive alternatives that will truly support people's

ideals and dreams. Organizations can benefit from the process by finding new directions for development, and learning new ways to respond to people.

What do we know about supporting positive outcomes?

The most powerful outcomes of futures planning emerge through the stories that people themselves tell when they feel they are active in creating life experiences that reflect their own interests and when they have a growing support group of interested, committed, and effective people who provide both emotional and instrumental assistance. They report a growing sense of optimism and hope as the process of change unfolds. Two powerful stories of change appear in Ducharme, Beeman, DeMarasse, & Ludlum (1994).

The stories of greatest change have shown that there are a number of conditions that strengthen the potential for positive outcomes. For example, personal and organizational support significantly increase the likelihood that a vision can be realized. Listed below are ten conditions concerning a variety of factors that strengthen and nurture the power of a plan and the likelihood that it will result in positive change (Mount, 1991a).

1. Positive change is more likely when the person, parents, or committed advocates want it and the energy is focused by a clear set of values and assumptions. When at least one person feels stuck in the current situation, is aware of other options, and has the energy for change, there will probably be more effectiveness.

2. People need the opportunity to see themselves in light of their gifts and capacities. This view is more likely to be maintained when a group of people develop a shared appreciation of the capacities of the person, and work together over time to develop and support these capacities.

3. The individual needs a specific personal vision for a different life. This vision is more likely to lead to change when it is sensitive to individual interests and local community life.

4. A group of people should be willing to meet on a regular basis to solve problems over time on behalf of the focus person. This support group (also called circle of support or person-centered team) develops a shared appreciation of the capacities and desires of the focus person and works together to identify obstacles and solve problems.

5. A skilled facilitator should be available to support a group over time. Under ideal conditions, an effective facilitator not only supports individual circles of support, but also builds the conditions that lead to change.

6. The support group should include at least one person, unpaid or paid, with a strong commitment to act on behalf of the person. This person(s) takes a very active role in making emergent ideas reality and may be a parent, friend, community member, service provider, group facilitator, or the focus person.

7. The support network should include at least one person who builds connections and opens doors in the local community. This community builder is often deeply rooted in the local neighborhood and community and knows how to create opportunities and support there.

8. It is helpful for the focus person to be connected to other people facing similar obstacles or, challenges. This network may be formal or informal, such as a group of parents concerned about inclusive education, residential options, and so forth.

9. At least one human service agency must be willing to change to support a person's dreams. Organizations providing flexible, individualized supports to help people realize their personal dreams are most effective. These individualized forms of support give control directly to those using the support.

10. The person should have access to people who make major decisions about resources at the local, regional, or state level. Influence with those in authority helps people express their issues and work constructively to find alternatives to existing limitations.

In keeping with the conditions listed above many of the agencies most interested in using a personal futures planning approach are innovative by nature. Staff in these agencies have a strong value base, a critical understanding of the nature of human services (Wolfensberger, 1983), and a powerful vision (O'Brien & Lyle, 1987). Many successful stories of change emerge from small agencies that use person-centered planning to support a radical conversion from segregated settings to individualized supports (Mount, 1987).

Other dramatic stories of change result from the intense advocacy efforts of a family member, the person with a disability, or a committed friend or ally (Mount & Caruso, 1989). Equally compelling outcomes occur when planners have access to substantial, flexible, individualized, packages of funding that can be used to finance the supports needed to realize a dream (Brost & Johnson, 1982; Mount, O'Brien, & Jacob, 1991). Some of the most moving stories of change occur when community members take a leadership role in realizing a vision (Mount, Ducharme, & Beeman, 1991). The most powerful change comes through people, communities, and organizations that are pursuing a powerful vision, that value strengthening and building personal supports, and that offer a variety of organizational incentives to facilitate the planning process.

In contrast, many organizational environments lack the conditions that nourish the implementation of a plan. Efforts to replicate the positive benefits of personal futures planning in these settings may be far less successful and can even backfire, causing people to feel disappointed, powerless, and cynical about innovation. Potential planners should proceed with a great deal of caution to avoid the most common implementation problems. Potential futures planners must work at the organizational and community level to increase the activities and investments that strengthen the power of an individual plan. The following section presents an overview of typical implementation problems, followed by a model for effective implementation.

Common breakdowns in implementation

Personal futures planning is least effective when it is used in isolation from other complementary change activities. This fragmentation is most likely to occur if the futures planning process is standardized, implemented on a large scale, or otherwise molded to fit into existing structures of service instead of challenging them.

The usefulness of personal futures planning is most often undermined by its popularity. The power of the initial planning process is seductive and entices people to implement the process for as many people as possible and train a host of others to do so as well. The following sections show the most common problems that occur in interpretation and implementation.

Seduction of the Quick Fix

The most common breakdown in the futures planning process occurs when people place too much emphasis on the initial meetings and do not value, plan, and invest in the ongoing process of follow-up and renewal. The first several meetings are powerful, and people are energized by describing the capacities of people and creating a vision together. But then comes the hard work of making the ideas a reality and slogging through the details, obstacles, and frustrations of implementation. Planners can attend more to follow-up when they limit the number of plans they initiate and work to create an organizational climate that builds the capacity to respond.

Grandiosity

Often when people are investing in planning meetings without attention to follow-up, they are also indulging in another undermining practice, that is, doing too many plans for too many people. This error is quite common because it is natural to think that if something is helpful, offering it to everyone make sense. It goes against a sense of equity and justice to single out a few people who will benefit initially. But it is important to trust that an effective, small-scale effort ultimately will benefit many people.

Standardization and Efficiency

Another common breakdown in the futures planning process occurs when people seek to streamline, mandate, and/or standardize the process to meet the system's demand for compliance, control, accountability, and efficiency. When the system takes over the futures planning process, the activity immediately loses its power, flexibility, and responsiveness, quickly becoming one more intrusive, insensitive, and ineffective activity. When people lacking strong person-centered values are given the power to conduct a procedure that has no potential to change the system of which it is a part, then futures planning becomes one more way to process people through a series of empty and meaningless rituals. There is a long way to go before organizational cultures have the capacity to plan thoughtfully for many people. In the meantime, it makes sense to provide personal futures planning as a planning option, as part of an integrated set of innovation activities. It makes sense to train interested and committed people to lead innovative efforts. Effective implementation on a small scale truly can change the way of thinking about being effective in the lives of all people (Mount et al., 1991).

Fragmentation from Organizational Change

The most common problem of personal futures planning occurs when the individual planning process is detached from the effort to change existing organizational structures, processes, and cultures. In order for staff within an agency to have the time, energy, money, and flexibility to respond to people, organizations must change, and the process of change is complex. In order for community members to be invited to participate in a person's life, someone has to do the asking and provide the support. Increasing numbers of people need to be freed up, sheltered, and supported to do this work (Landis & Peeler, 1990).

People who plan for positive futures must be prepared to respond to the person, explore the community, and work to change the system to obtain free spaces in which people can respond and life can evolve. When futures planning is separated from the process of organizational change, ironically, it is harder to maintain the free spaces and flexibility in which the most lively change occurs. *Framework for Accomplishment* (O'Brien & Lyle O'Brien 1987), presents lessons and tools to help people develop some skills to bridge the gap between person-centered planning and organizational change.

There are some exceptions to the need for organizational support. For example, some people using the futures planning process are not dependent on human services systems and do not plan to be. They can avoid the challenge of organizational change by working exclusively to build informal supports, and this is an admirable effort. However, most people do not have the choice of working totally outside the boundaries of human services organizations.

Consequences of using personal futures planning in a system-centered way

Person-centered planning is least effective when it is implemented in a system-centered way. Systems rely on big numbers, magnify promises of change, and are driven by standardization and efficiency. System-centered change, likewise, is constrained by these qualities.

Fortunately, there are ways to safeguard the positive aspects of personal futures planning when it is integrated with a number of other renewing and innovative activities. These person-centered development projects create a safe haven from the demands of system-centered work and allow staff to learn how to think and respond in different ways. As people learn new ways of taking action, this knowledge begins to filter into larger systems and into the collective consciousness of possibility. This is a more effective way to spread the benefits of the futures planning approach. Some aspects of effective person-centered development are discussed in the following section.

A learning process approach

Learning about person-centered development comes from a variety of projects that integrate ongoing renewal activities with an implementation design that enables people to listen, test their ideals, learn new skills, make new investments, and measure success. These innovative projects are replacing a reliance on rules, regulations, and bureaucracy as the way to organize work. They create an alternative learning process that supports creativity, reflection, collaborative problem-solving, and personal learning that leads to change (Korten, 1983).

At the level of the individual, community, agency, region, or state, each project invests in five closely linked activities, each of which makes a contribution to helping people think and respond differently. If an organization cannot invest in each learning activity, personal futures planning alone is likely to become an empty ritual. Following are descriptions of these activities (O'Brien & Mount, 1988).

Personal futures planning provides an important opportunity for renewal within an agency. The process brings people together to develop images of desirable individual futures and collaborative strategies for realizing them. The process is adapted to fit the mission, the people, and the community. Four additional complementary activities that provide opportunities for learning and renewal are listed below:

1. *Interactive problem solving* involves small groups of people in creative management of the day-to-day problems of taking constructive action on personal futures planning and redesign efforts.
2. *Strategic redesign* entails investing a growing proportion of the organization's time and money in developing new community opportunities, creating new connections and roles for people, and supporting people's continuing participation.
3. *Systematic evaluation* ensures review of the effectiveness and efficiency of organizational changes.
4. *Structured reflection* provides occasions for those involved in changes to deepen their understanding of the ethical issues at stake in delivering responsible services to people who are socially devalued.

As individual support groups and/or organizations increase their investment in these activities, they are able to develop unique responses that increase the fit between the interests and gifts of people with disabilities on the one hand, and community opportunities and system resources on the other. These designs for support cannot simply be invented and imposed by hierarchical, standardized, bureaucratic processes. Direction for change must emerge from groups of people who listen to each other, respond, solve problems, reflect, and redesign services so they have more time, energy, and money to respond to people's needs.

The learning approach is different from standard operating procedure because it challenges people to develop and act on their own knowledge of the grassroots, which ultimately diminishes their reliance on the often meaningless demands of external authorities. It makes sense to build this learning capacity on a small scale and expand as people increase their ability to work in a completely different way. The following section outlines the key components of person-centered development projects that can shelter the free space needed for innovation.

Person-centered development projects

Effective person-centered projects not only rely on a number of renewal activities for direction, they also include a process for learning about implementation, developing effective leadership, ensuring outcomes in people's lives, and changing organizations as needed. All of these activities are linked and integrated in an intentional design for learning. While these projects vary greatly in their scale, location, intent, leadership, and organizational environments, they share the following characteristics:

1. *Beginning with a focus question:* A focus is found by clarifying an issue or challenge that needs exploration, for example:
   - Providing more options for the transition out of high school
   - Dealing with behaviors that challenge existing environments
   - Owning a residence
   - Including children fully in neighborhood schools
2. *Convening a study group:* A small collective of people who have a stake in the focus question and want to be part of finding new solutions should be identified. This group often includes a facilitator, a change agent, the person with a disability, and a person from an executive area.
3. *Creating a listening body:* A place for innovation that is sheltered from the demands and requirements of the existing system

should be designed. This listening body should have the four aspects listed below:

- A limited number of people with disabilities whose lives will inform the focus question and who want to be involved in the process of exploration
- Facilitators who take the lead in learning to conduct futures plans and provide follow-up
- Support circles or groups to provide day-to-day and ongoing support to the focus person
- The support of a representative from management who can respond with administrative flexibility and support

4. *Providing opportunities for renewal:* Ongoing occasions for people to obtain new ideas and reflect and deepen their values and commitment must be ensured.

5 *Planning regular forums/meetings with organizational stake holders:* Members of the listening body should meet, as needed, to identify themes in the process of implementation and develop platforms for change that suggest concrete alternatives of what would be better. Members then meet in person with critical organizational stakeholders to discuss issues and work out solutions.

A person-centered development project draws some boundaries around a small number of people, facilitators, administrators, and community members so that they have the support to plan with people and see their ideas to fruition. As ideals are implemented, people grow in their sense of accomplishment and their personal and group authority and capacity to make good things happen. These positive approaches and outcomes then begin to spread to others, and new development projects are initiated.

The limits have been reached on the system-centered approach to people with disabilities and their families, which worked through rationality, efficiency, and equality. Person-centered development is a more organic approach. Personal futures planning is one of a number of person-centered planning approaches that strengthen the capacity to see people differently and to develop a vision that leads to powerful change. However, thinking differently is just the beginning of change. A wonderful personal futures plan is only one aspect of a number of innovative and renewing activities that help interested people learn new ways to respond. It is a helpful tool in the hands of committed people who work in a environment ripe for change. Planners interested in the futures planning approach must look beyond the lure of the quick fix of the initial planning meetings toward the long journey of learning to do things differently on personal, community, and organizational levels. The resources of the system can be used to support safe havens where people can learn the art of person-centered development. The continuing challenge is to create environments in which the nurturing needed for the concern, commitment, and caring that engenders true relationships can be given.

References

Brost, M., & Johnson, T. (1982). *Getting to know you.* Madison, WI: Wisconsin Coalition for Advocacy.

Forest, M. & Snow, J. (1987). *The MAPS process.* Toronto: Frontier College.

Green, K. (1984). Twenty-four hour planning for persons with complex needs. *Canadian Journal on Mental Retardation, 34*(1), 3–11.

Korten, D. (1983). People-centered development: Toward a framework. In D. Korten & E. Klauss (Eds.), *People-centered development: Contributions toward theory and planning frameworks.* West Hartford, CT: Kumarian Press.

Landis, S. & Peeler, J. (1990). *What have we noticed as we've tried to assist people one person at a time?* Chillicothe, OH: Ohio Safeguards.

Mount, B. (1987). *Personal futures planning. Finding directions for change.* University of Michigan Dissertation Service.

Mount, B. (1991a). *Dare to dream. An analysis of the conditions that lead to personal change for people with disabilities.* Manchester, CT: Communitas.

Mount, B. (1991b). *Person-centered planning: A sourcebook of values, ideals and method to encourage person-centered development.* New York: Graphic Futures.

Mount, B. & Caruso, G. (1989). *New dreams, new lives, new directions for alternative living, Inc.* Annapolis, MD: Alternative Living Inc.

Mount, B., Ducharme, G., & Beeman, P (1991). *Person-centered development: A journey in learning to listen to people with disabilities*. Manchester, CT: Communitas.

Mount, B., Lyle O'Brien, C., & Jacob, G. (1991). *New vision, new challenges: Reflections on the challenges of person-centered residential service development*. Annapolis, MD: Alternative Living, Inc.

O'Brien, J. (1987). A guide to life-style planning: Using The Activities Catalog to integrate services and natural support systems. In B. Wilcox & G. T Bellamy (Eds.), *A comprehensive guide to The Activities Catalog: An alternative curriculum for youth and adults with severe disabilities* (pp. 175—189). Baltimore. MD: Paul H. Brookes Publishing Co.

O'Brien, J. & Lyle O'Brien, C. (1987). *Framework for accomplishment*. Lithonia, GA: Responsive Systems Associates.

O'Brien, J. & Mount, B. (1988). *Person-centered development: Thinking tool*. Lithonia, GA: Responsive Systems Associates.

Wolfensberger, W. (1983). Social role valorization: A proposed new term for the principle of normalization. *Mental Retardation, 21*(6), 234–239

9

The Quest for Community Membership

John O'Brien & Connie Lyle O'Brien

> *...we must inescapably understand our lives*
> *in narrative form, as a 'quest'.*
> – Charles Taylor (1989)

How can person-centered planning contribute to building communities competent to include people with developmental disabilities
as contributing members? Failure to actively and thoughtfully engage this tough question unnecessarily limits the effectiveness of the
growing variety of approaches to person-centered planning as a set
of tools for social change.

The image of a quest –a difficult search through unknown territory for something that seems good to the hero– provides a way to
think about the relationship between person-centered planning and
community building. Whether it concerns Rama's search for his
kidnapped wife Sita, Odessus' voyage home, Perceval's pursuit of the
Holy Grail, or Judith Snow's quest for the kind of personal assistance that frees her from imprisonment in a nursing home (Pearpoint, 1990), the story of a quest answers at least four questions:

- What does the hero seek?
- Who are the hero's companions?
- What are the challenges and aids offered by the territory through
  which the hero journeys and what prices must the hero pay to
  continue the journey?
- How does the quest change the hero?

Each of these questions opens a window on the effectiveness of
person-centered planning. We will look through just one of these
windows by asking about the nature of the territory indicated by a
person-centered plan. Where does the person-centered planning
process point the focus person and their allies? What sort of social
space does the process suggest as the places to encounter unknown
troubles on the search for what seems good? Obviously, particular
answers to this question matter most: in which specific places and
among which specific people within reach might this particular

person find what matters most to her at this time in her life? But practitioners of person-centered planning can learn something by taking a step back and considering which of three types of social spaces the plans they facilitate encourage focus people and their allies to travel through.

John McKnight (1995) introduced us to the idea of social spaces and their important effects on social policy, though he can't be held responsible for the use we make of it here. McKnight points out many disadvantages of making policy based on a too simple map of social life, a map that nowadays too often excludes the associations that people create when they assume shared responsibility for naming and solving their own problems together and highlights either bureaucratic structures or individualistic pursuits as the primary source of good things. Ignoring associations generates policies that weaken communities by directing resources into bureaucracies or private pockets and discouraging people from working together to claim their own difficulties and the opportunities those difficulties create.

While person-centered planning makes only a modest difference to community building compared with policies that sink billions of dollars into programs that segregate and control people with disabilities, we think it's worthwhile for person-centered planners to make this modest difference: both for the real benefits to the people involved and for the lessons their experience can teach whatever policy makers have ears to hear them. So we suggest that person-centered planners review their work by asking. "Do the plans I facilitate focus people's attention primarily on managed space or private space or do they lead people to continue further on to explore and strengthen shared space?"

It's important to acknowledge how difficult it is to make any significant and lasting change for people with developmental disabilities. The social forces that drive segregation and control exert a powerful pull on people's lives. One committed staff member describes it this way,

> It almost seems like we travel around in an invisible
> bubble. Like at church: people were nervous at first but
> now they are nice enough, they smile and say 'Hi', or even
> chat for a minute, but we're still inside the bubble and they
> are outside it. And it's all so fragile. When he had a stroke
> a few months ago, the system tried to move him into a
> nursing home.

Any quest that overcomes this dismal history of segregation and control deserves honor, regardless of which social space people journey through. However, work to change shared space offers the greatest opportunity for learning about how person-centered planning can encourage people to break through the invisible bubble. So we hope that each practitioner of person-centered planning supports at least one or two focus people whose quests draw them into shared space.

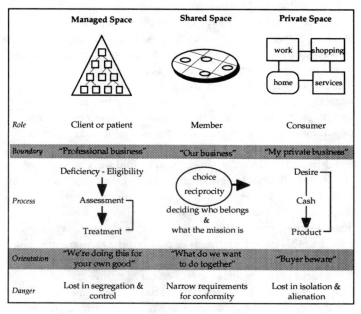

	Managed Space	Shared Space	Private Space
Role	Client or patient	Member	Consumer
Boundary	"Professional business"	"Our business"	"My private business"
Process	Deficiency - Eligibility → Assessment → Treatment	choice reciprocity / deciding who belongs & what the mission is	Desire → Cash → Product
Orientation	"We're doing this for your own good"	"What do we want to do together"	"Buyer beware"
Danger	Lost in segregation & control	Narrow requirements for conformity	Lost in isolation & alienation

A quest that stays in **managed space** is a search for more comfortable clienthood or more powerful professional interventions. It does not disturb the physical and social distance that separates people with disabilities. It asks for better use of the professional authority over people built into program structures. The quest concludes when service workers adjust what they do to better accommodate the person within a service. Assisting a much anticipated trip to Disneyland, adjusting staff's routine to better accommodate a person's preferences, winning funding for a power wheelchair, or getting approval for a transfer from an activity center to supported employment could each be worthy goals of a quest that stays in managed space. The challenges on a journey in managed space include: programs designed with the assumption that people will adjust to fit them, inflexible readings of regulations and budgets, and staff fear that change might involve heightened liability, or conflict, or inconvenience. Help will come from staff members and managers who identify with the focus person's desire and decide to create the flexibility to accommodate it.

Partly in reaction to dependence on staff benevolence for journeys in managed space, some reformers join person-centered planning to self-determination, a system change that increases people's control of an individual service budget. This puts the focus person in the role of service consumer and sets free the inventiveness of journeys in **private space**. In this space, the key question is, "How do you want to live (given the limits of your budget and the kinds of supports that are on offer)?" A journey that stays in private space finishes when the customer is satisfied enough with the service product to close negotiations. This shift in the balance of power creates new responsibilities: the consumer must become informed enough to have a basis for evaluating and negotiating a service provider's offer and delivered services; the consumer must find ways to stretch or adjust the individual budget when the cost of their requirements for assistance changes; the consumer must become an effective employer of support workers; the consumer must decide how to live. These journeys challenge allies about when and how to try to influence the focus person's decisions or confront the focus person about apparent problems. Help comes in the form of small breakthroughs as the focus person realizes the excitement of having and solving daily problems. Help comes when the focus person and their allies and the people who provide assistance recognize their interdependence as a source for creative problem solving. Help comes as difficulties give people the occasion to live up to their trust in one another.

Quests into **shared space** usually pass through managed space or private space, but they don't stop when services improve or customers are satisfied. Travelers in shared space search for understanding of the gifts a person can contribute to the common good and for opportunities to make those contributions. This search attends to who a person becomes beyond being a client or a consumer, to what a person wants to use their freedom for. This sort of quest may sound a bit grand, but usually it is simple enough. A passion for nature leads to a semi-formal group that spends Saturday mornings cleaning up a polluted creek. Curiosity about sailing boats leads to membership in a society dedicated to restoring and preserving old boats. Concern for homeless people leads to week after week of volunteer work in a shelter kitchen. A family heritage of making church music leads to a place in the choir. A gift of hospitality leads to dinner parties that gather and expand groups of friends. Hunger for justice leads to a job organizing people with disabilities. Interest in local politics leads to hours of envelope stuffing. Some challenges on journeys in shared space arise in refining understanding of the person's gifts, especially when those gifts are buried by years of low expectations and imposed passivity. Help with these challenges will come from imaginative listeners who are willing to check their intuitions by inviting and supporting the focus person to try something new. Other challenges come in arranging the assistance a person needs to participate: getting rides, assuring that a person has the help necessary to be up and dressed on time, and making room in the schedule for a person's memberships. Help here will come in the form of service workers who are willing to join in the quest. Still other challenges come as people cross the boundaries that form the invisible bubbles that can contain even a person who is present to community life. Help in these negotiations will come from people whose sense of hospitality and appreciation of a person's contribution draws them past unfamiliarity and awkwardness into mutuality. Not everyone who wants a person-centered plan will want to undertake a quest in shared space. But the more ready facilitators become to join in building community, the more people they will find ready to join them.

References

McKnight, J. (1995). *The careless society: Community and its counterfeits.* New York: Basic Books.

Pearpoint, J. (1990). *From behind the piano: The building of Judith Snow's unique circle of friends.* Toronto: Inclusion Press.

Taylor, C. (1989). *Sources of the self.* Cambridge, MA: Harvard University Press. Page 52.

10

After the Plan

Michael W. Smull

Learning how people want to live and then doing nothing with the information is a form of abuse. A good plan not only clarifies what each individual wants but creates the perception that those who participated in the planning will do something about it. Planning should only occur where there is a commitment to implement. The challenge in implementation is where to start. The disparity between how people want to live and how they are living often creates a feeling of being overwhelmed, of not knowing where or how to start. The following is an effort to assist those who are engaged in this struggle and to reduce implementation to its essential elements. The process is outlined in this flow chart.

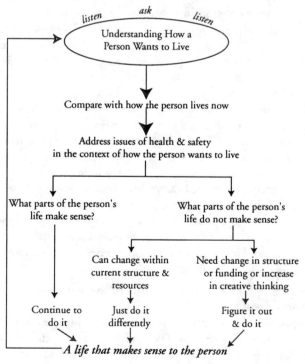

Learning how people want to live

The process of implementation of a person centered plan begins with learning how people want to live through a structured process of asking and listening. Honest planning is never finished. People continue to grow and change. As what is important to them changes and as our understanding continues to deepen, the plans should change. Plans are a snapshot of how someone wants to live today, serving as a blueprint for how to support someone tomorrow. They need to be written down so that we have a benchmark of how people want to live. Honest plans also reflect how each individual wants to live, not how we think they should live. Plans should reflect the typically modest wishes and desires of the person and not represent fantasy of the "good life" from the person doing the planning. Person centered planning can be learned by reading and practicing but it is easier (and safer for people with disabilities) to learn from others who have been trained.

Continuously considering issues of health and safety

Doing person centered planning does not relieve us of the obligation to address issues of health and safety. People who are unusually vulnerable need to have safeguards and people with medical needs must have adequate health care. The challenge is to consider these issues within the context of how the person wants to live. In the flow chart this is shown as occurring after the comparison between how people want to live and how they are living. Its presence near the top of the process is in part symbolic. In careful implementation, issues of health and safety are not considered only once, they are continuously considered. The challenge in implementation is to enhance safety and ensure health without compromising those things that are important to the person. Once there is an understanding of how the person wants to live, any compromises in what is important to the person are made consciously, after efforts have been made to think of how the person can have what is important and still be safe and healthy.

Comparing how the person wants to live with how the person is living

Comparing how people want to live with how they are living is a form of discrepancy analysis. The result creates the agenda for action. Knowing what is important to a person (and knowing how important it is) is followed by looking at how the person is living now and determining to what degree each of these things is present or absent. Careful consideration of the difference between what people want and what they have shows what parts of their lives make sense and what parts do not.

Giving credit for what is working well

It is important to not only highlight the need for change but to highlight those things that are being done well and acknowledging those things that are being done that do make sense (and continuing to do them). There is an unfortunate tendency to wallow in blame and guilt when the discrepancies are seen between what is important to the people and how we have been supporting them. A sense of urgency is needed but guilt is not helpful. Rhonda's story illustrates these issues. How Rhonda was being supported Monday through Friday reflected a deep caring and understanding of how she wanted to live. Although she does not use words to talk, staff who loved her were listening to her behavior and honoring her positive rituals and choices. As a person-centered plan was developed with Rhonda, it became clear that the weekend staff did not know her as well and were not listening. The reaction of the people who supported Rhonda during the week was dismay and determination. They were pleased at how much they knew and dismayed at how it was not being used help Rhonda on the weekends. Talking about what was going well validated the efforts of the direct care staff who loved Rhonda and were listening to her. Looking at the discrepancy reframed what had been seen as her "behavior problems" on week-ends into a problem with the support she was being given. It gave a sense of direction.

Changes that can be made within current structures and resources

Rhonda's life also provides an example of how needed changes can occur within current structure and resources. Planning with Rhonda made it clear that she must be supported by people who are calm, soft spoken and not "in her face". She must be supported by people who understand how she communicates with her behavior, who listen to what she is saying. Some of the people supporting her on the weekends were not calm or soft spoken and tended to "get in her face". They were the wrong people to support Rhonda. They were not "bad" people, it was a bad match. With some rearranging of where people worked Rhonda began to have weekend support that made sense to her. The staff who know Rhonda also developed a "cheat sheet" that told how to interpret what Rhonda was saying with her behavior. For example, everyone who supports Rhonda now knows she tells you when she wants to get up in the morning by being on her stomach, propped up on her elbows. Her "problem behavior" is gone and someone who was labeled "nonverbal" is now described as "outspoken".

Changes that require changes in current structures or resources

Some of the issue's in Harry's life illustrate how some changes can be made immediately while others will take time and require changes in structure. Harry will not eat with people that he dislikes and shares his house with a roommate whom he strongly dislikes. He does like eating in his room, by himself. Using typical "group home thinking" staff used to say: "We eat family style and we all eat together." As staff learned about choice they were willing to support Harry eating in his room except that it would not be "fair" to another roommate. Harry had another roommate who liked to store food in his room. Staff felt that they could not want to let Harry do something that another person in the house could not do. They did not feel that fellow who "hoarded" food could be allowed to eat in his room because it would create a health issue as perishable food aged. In trying to honor choice, staff were saying that Harry did not have to eat with everyone, but there were no inhome alternatives. Harry could, and often does, eat with friends and relatives who live elsewhere, but he was also simply not eating some nights.

When we did the planning with Harry, the fellow who stored food in his room had moved, so "fairness" was no longer an issue. (If that roommate had been present the argument would have been made that treating everyone the same in this circumstance is inherently unfair.) As the issues for Harry were reviewed, it was clear that supporting Harry in eating in his room made sense. Harry left the planning meeting with a "dining" table for his room (that had been stored in the basement) and was going home to have supper in his room. The staff who support Harry had committed to find a way for Harry to only live with people that he chose (and liked). However, helping Harry move requires that the agency figure out the finances involved in closing the group home. While this will take time, in the interim Harry will be happier and will eat regularly.

Harry's story also brings up an issue of health. Since Harry has no unusual medical issues skipping an occasional meal is not a problem. The concern is that he would skip enough meals to unbalance his nutrition and/or to cause him to lose too much weight. Harry does not have enough money to eat out all the time and he does not eat with his friends every night. He was skipping enough meals to have a noticeable weight loss (although not enough to raise immediate health concerns). Neither depression nor an eating disorder seemed to be needed to explain his not eating at home. Hating one of his roommates and having no alternative appeared to be sufficient explanation. Eating in his room is the temporary solution. He still eats out as he can afford it, and he eats with friends and relatives as often as he is invited.

A life that makes sense to the individual

The desired outcome is a life that makes sense to the individual. How each person wants to live should be congruent with how they are living. This does not mean that everyone gets everything that they want. Some things are beyond our power to provide, some things take time, and some things cost more than we can afford A women I met in Chicago told me that the only living situation acceptable to her was to live with her mother. Unfortunately, her mother made it clear that regardless of the supports offered she was not prepared for her daughter to return home. To help this women achieve a life that makes sense we have to help her deal with the loss of her home with her mother and to develop other relationships.

Many of those things that are important to people take time to achieve. For people living in group settings, the changes that are possible will not work for everyone. If you hate one of your roommates, not having to eat in the same room helps. However, it does not address the underlying issue that you should be able to pick who you live with. Because sites are funded rather than people, because having one or two people move may leave a deficit that cannot be covered, helping people leave group settings takes time. Moving to a new place requires that we not only know how people want to live but how we can pay for it. Where group homes are being closed, disposing of the building may require significant effort. Helping people leave group homes can be done and should be done, but it does take time.

Many people say that they want to live by themselves. This is the request that most often challenges the disability system. The easiest way to control costs is to share them. By requiring that people share housing and staff, costs are reduced. Where people live by themselves this economy is absent. If everyone wanted to live by themselves the disability system would never be able to bear the cost. However, if only a small percent want to live by themselves at any one time it should be affordable. Many people want to try living by themselves, but only a few people like it as a permanent way of life. Further, many people have been forced to share their lives with their roommates and need to experience what just sharing space is like. (When you share lives you do everything together, when you share space you sleep in the same house and otherwise select what you do together.)

Home ownership is another example of something that appears too costly. The disability system has made it possible for agencies to own thousands of houses but sees home ownership for individuals as too expensive. It does take time, knowledge, and commitment but people across the United States and Canada are finding ways to buy their own homes. It is only too costly when it is seen as something which should be solely financed by the disability system.

Home ownership is also an example of a dream. Whenever a dream for the future is expressed there are a few questions that should be asked. The first question to ask is whose dream is this? Most people need to have a life before they begin to have dreams of things like owning their own home. Check and see if it is really their dream, or is it the dream that the facilitator thought they should have. If it is their dream, does it really need to happen tomorrow, or is it something to work toward? Simple dreams like living only with people that I like, only being supported by people that I trust, or having privacy in the bathroom, should be achieved quickly. Expensive dreams, extraordinary dreams, which are the person's and not the product of a guided fantasy, become something that the person should be supported in working toward.

Remember to keep listening

Whenever people are empowered a dynamic situation is created. The process of listening and then acting on what has been heard is an ongoing cycle. What people want today will be different from what they want tomorrow. The process is lifelong and interactive.

The only thing worse than never listening is only listening once. The process should continuously loop back, comparing how people are living with how they want to live. Where there are differences a plan needs to be developed to help the individual to continue the pursuit of happiness.

11

Participation Through Support Circles

Judith A. Snow

Most people who work in a professional capacity vis á vis people who have been labeled handicapped have been shaped and trained into viewing handicap as the focus of their efforts. Regardless of what one's role is, disability is the reason for its existence. If one does therapy it is because a circumstance limits the client's physical or mental functioning. If one finds residential placements it is because the client has a limitation leading to a need for unusual support in typical daily activities. Even if one is an advocate it is because the presence of disability in a person's mind and/or body often puts that person at risk of negative social circumstances.

Most family members and friends of people who acquire disability labels are shaped by our surrounding culture to adopt similar approaches.

This simple fact leads into the greatest dilemma facing people everywhere who are, or who work with, or who care about people labeled disabled. That dilemma is captured by the slogans adopted world wide by people who live with these labels: "Label jars not people." and, "Call us People First."

Even those who try consistently and faithfully to relate to people as people find that disability inescapably remains at the core of most interactions. The very nature of our culturally given perception of disability and our response to it seems to obscure our perception of the people behind the labels. What can a concerned person do?

You may find that by becoming a circle builder you may find an opportunity to actually make a difference in the lives of some people.

Support circles break through the disability focus in several ways. Most significantly, circles are powerful because they exist to honor, support and make available a person's capacities and interests, not his or her deficits. Support circles are formed to be vehicles for people to discover and to talk about ways in which a person could be contributing to the wider community through, often overlooked, interests and talents. They struggle to communicate to a wider world what capacity the focus person has to enrich others. They discover or create places, supports and contacts that will make this person's participation grow and develop.

Secondly, support circles are powerful because their focus is on relationships and not individuals. Circles function primarily by bringing the focus person into a richer, more diverse network of listening people. The person's nature and ability is unfolded by the interactions fostered by the network. Disability loses its power to focus people's time and energy. Disability is disempowered.

A support circle belongs to the world of participation. Just the initial establishment of a circle is already a step forward to having someone participate in the community. The focus is on one person yet all the members of the circle typically will experience their participation in the circle as a vehicle for examining and improving their own contributions to society.

Although a support circle is not always necessary, it has a unique power for rapidly changing the life experience of an individual who is facing great barriers to participation. A circle is a creation in the area of relationship, meaning and interaction. People experience being part of a circle as 'natural' and they 'know' how to offer both formal and informal support to each other.

Circles also empower circle members and builders because they are unpredictable. Energized by multiple, complex relationships they often become magnets of synergy, taking advantage of lucky accidents —opportunities that cannot be predicted or bureaucratically managed into existence. This living essence of circles drives out the deadening spirit of disability thinking.

The lives of people who have been 'helped' are usually scarred by disrespect, physical and emotional abuse, and broken relationships. Often these wounds are the result of well-intentioned interventions. At the beginning and throughout, it is important to recognize that support circles have power —both to support or to hinder. The person who is interested in starting circles can still be drawn into disability as a focus. A personal discipline will help restrain them from doing this harm in a vulnerable person's life. This practice is outlined below.

Build a safe course by following these steps.

- Give up disability, its language and its forms. People are opportunities and people have opportunities to enrich community. Learn to see these.

- Practice inclusion to learn inclusion.
- Dream. Invite people to listen to your dreams.
- Listen to other people's dreams.
- Say "Yes".
- Listen.
- Give up doing what doesn't work.
- Invite diversity into your own life.
- Recruit a coach. Be a coach. Together support each other to learn circle building more deeply.

In the gathering of the circle the intention is established to listen to a person's dream and to create the resources and openings required to bring this person's dream into the community. The focus remains on the person who is vulnerable to being isolated and to being a nonparticipant.

The following are the steps required to create a support circle:

1. Figure out who the circle is for.
2. Invite.
3. Ensure that dreaming, story telling and listening happen at every circle meeting.
4. Keep the circle meeting.
5. Make sure that the focus person says 'Yes' to something that the circle offers.

First of all it can often be a little mind-bending figuring out who the circle is for. In the situation where the focus person is an adult who speaks for themselves the scenario is fairly straight forward. Such situations are rare. More typically one person is the named focus but the real focus is on a parent or an advocate who typically speaks for this person.

There is nothing wrong with a parent or an advocate being the focus. In fact when the circle involves children it is essential that the circle be formed around the parent(s). The issue is simply that when the focus is confused the process gets unclear and the action stalls. Therefore it is essential that this issue be sorted out, likely on many different occasions.

Occasionally the focus of the circle will shift for a short period of time. This is a good thing unless for some reason it is difficult to return the focus to the person the circle started for. In such a situation consider starting two circles that are interconnected by having some joint membership. This is a useful strategy in situations like a teacher with a vulnerable child in a regular classroom or a parent with a teenager who is vulnerable to being labeled. For example the teacher could have a circle of adults including the parents of the child and some of the child's classmates and the child could have a circle of children from the class and from the neighborhood.

Inviting is a critical stage often full of struggle. People typically say that they do not know anyone to invite. This is absolutely not true, yet in a certain sense the experience is quite real. After all, it is to be expected that the person's life is full of paid people and others focused on therapy and advocacy plus lots of other people who have been carefully trained by society to see this individual as limited and in need of fixing. The dynamics of the disability focus make it almost a certainty that all these people have been interacting in ways that push each other away. It doesn't occur to the individual in question that some of these very same people are able to and in fact would love to have an opportunity to foster participation.

Keeping the dreaming, story telling and listening alive is not difficult. Yet someone must always watch that dreams don't drop off the agenda. We have all been carefully trained to become busy planners and behavior police. Listen for dreaming, stories and listening and keep the circle going.

The job of keeping the circle meeting arises because circles typically experience either great success or unexpected overwhelming barriers right at the beginning. In either situation the disability focus teaches us to give up because if we have succeeded then the situation must have been fixed and if we have failed it must be unfixable. It usually takes time for people to catch the rhythm of dreaming, story telling and listening. In fact the person is included as soon as the circle begins to meet since it is the journey of interactions and meanings and the listening to dreams that counts much more than the outward successes. In time, as the circle experiences the invention of its own story and as successes emerge from unexpected directions, the issue of meeting will be less critical.

The point is that the support circle is the vehicle of listening to dream. The listening must continue until there are enough other possibilities of listening in the individual's relationship network. Even then, life is very fragile, and the circle may need to be called together if the ghost of 'disability' raises its head again.

Perhaps the biggest surprise will be in how much work there is in getting someone to say "Yes". In many subtle and devious ways people have learned to say "No". When a circle listens to dreaming, the listeners will begin to offer all sorts of opportunities and resources to the focus person. They do this because they are human and not because anyone asks them to. People will make suggestions of other people that might like to join the circle; they will offer to find jobs; they will offer to come and help out; they will offer to go to meetings or write letters; they will offer to make cookies; etc., etc., etc. And the focus person will say "No" to it all. They will say "No" because it is the wrong people; They will say "No" because it's the wrong job; they will say "No" because they can do it better themselves; they will say "No" because they don't like cookies; etc., etc., etc.

Saying "No" is a behavior encouraged by disability focus. People don't realize that No limits possibility and that giftedness can only grow out of Yes. In the world of participation the decision to say "No" must be taken only after careful reflection and because there is a boundary to possibility that you want to make. It is the facilitator's job to get people to say "Yes".

In summary, circle building is a five step process liberating a person's participation in community. Like all simple things in life, there is an underlying integrity which must be honored if support circles are to be effective. This integrity requires a commitment to give up disability and its focus on fixing people.

Building relationships, building participation and building community take time and commitment. They are a slow process that often takes years to reach full fruition. Yet, paradoxically, participation and relationship are the road to truly supporting vulnerable people. Nothing else works.

12

A Circle Check-Up

John O'Brien & Jeff Strully*

For the past four years, circles of support have been a key element in developing and guiding the supported living program operated by Jay Nolen Community Services (JNCS) in Los Angeles. Initially responsible for designing and implementing each individual's move from group home life into their own home, each person's circle now manages the person's support system and makes and implements long term plans. This shift of responsibility from agency to circles moves family members from being monitors of a group home to being directors of a personalized support system. It moves staff from being in charge of a group of clients to participating with circle members in designing and offering the supports and services a person requires to live successfully in their own home and participate in community life in satisfying ways.

The people JNCS supports count on their circles for the safety and quality of their daily lives. Only a few people currently have communication systems adequate to allow them an unambiguous voice in stating their dreams or directing their supports. Circle members hold responsibility for developing a deep, accurate, and clear account of the person's interests, preferences, and dreams and assuring that this understanding guides day to day staff behavior. People will require a highly organized support system for the rest of their lives. Circle members hold responsibility for extending continuity through the person's lifetime by clarifying and supporting the commitments necessary to the person's security. Prejudice, widespread confusion about the nature of autism, and a history of segregated services leave people at great risk of isolation. Circle members hold responsibility for expanding the circle's membership and supporting and challenging the person to expand the network of those who know and care about him or her. Many barriers stand in the way of pursuing simple things, like living comfortably or having a job; and, keeping the supported living program focused on individual needs

---

* This paper is based on a discussion with family members, friends, and JNCS staff involved in circles of support held on 27 April 1997

can call for the most assertive and creative negotiation with the service system that funds and regulates supported living. Circle members hold responsibility for persistent, creative problem solving, and vigorous representation of the person's interests. People are vulnerable to changes in their own condition, changes in the lives of the people who are critical to them, changes in their support system, and changes in the policies and programs that fund and provide the assistance they depend on. Circle members hold responsibility for sticking with the person through crises in order to protect the person's interests.

From time to time, a circle can use these key questions as a way to check up on their stewardship of these vital responsibilities.

- How have we strengthened our relationship with the person at the center of the circle?
  - What have we learned about accommodating the person so that we are better able to understand him or her; and so that he or she is better able to participate in the work of the circle?
  - What assumptions about the person's preferences, interests, or abilities have we revised? What have we been wrong in believing about the person? What differences have those of us who are closest to the person discovered between our own preferences, interests, and values and those of the person?
  - How have we shared the person's life outside the formal work of the circle?
- How has our shared knowledge about the person's identity and desirable future grown? What has becomes less certain about the future and what has become more clear to us?
  - What have we agreed to invest in for the person's long term future?
  - What have we discovered about what works to assist the person with life changes?
  - What have we done to deepen our understanding of the person?
  - What have we done to better organize our shared action?
- What actions have we taken that identify and deal with threats to the person's safety, comfort, and well being?
- What actions have we taken that stretch us outside our comfort zone?

- What has the circle put behind itself (for example, resentment at the responsibilities of circle membership, or fear of sharing dreams, or denial of unsatisfactory conditions)?
- What conflicts still get the circle stuck?
  - What do members see and believe that they are afraid to say? What circle business do people talk about outside the circle that doesn't get brought up with the whole circle?
  - What decisions does the circle try to avoid by passing them on to service agency authority?
  - What issues cause unproductive fights and cue disrespectful treatment of other circle members or supported living staff?
- How has the circle reached out to recruit new members and put them to work...
  ...from the person's family and extended family?
  ...from the larger community?
- What have we learned about achieving and maintaining an effective balance between the contributions of family and friends and the contributions of paid staff members?
- How have we become more effective as a group...
  ...by increasing our ability to speak openly and honestly when we disagree?
  ...by dealing more creatively with conflicts?
  ...by learning how to better understand members with different points of view?
  ...by finding ways to inquire more deeply into issues that keep coming up over and over again without resolution?
  ...by noticing when we fail to treat other members respectfully and making amends?
  ...by acknowledging our own ways of getting in the way of the circle's work and supporting one another to achieve self control?
- How have circle members increased their skills and knowledge...
  ...through participation in training related to values issues and positive practices?
  ...through research on how to make the systems that affect available opportunities work for the person?
  ...in discussion and exchange with members of other circles?
  ...by learning ways to improve the effectiveness of the circle as a creative problem solving group?

A circle may want to choose one of these questions and take time to discuss it at a regular circle meeting, or a circle could set aside a meeting for reflection on some of these questions with an outside facilitator, or circle members could pick some of the questions and ask an outsider to interview circle members individually and report the results for discussion. What matters most is building honest reflection into the work of the circle.

13

The Ethics of MAPS and PATH

Jack Pearpoint & Marsha Forest

You make the path by walking

Dilemmas, definitions, MAPS and PATH

Along with our colleagues at the Centre for Integrated Education and Community, we developed MAPS and PATH and had been using them for several years when some people started to refer to them as "person centered planning" tools. To understand this new way of naming what we have created, we resorted to the *Random House College Dictionary*.

person: a human being

centered: to be focused on

planning: a method of action or procedure, a design, a drawing, a map or diagram for the future

Person-centered planning –three wonderful words. No jargon. Very straightforward. The planning is centered on the person. Simple and yet profound. For us that means the planning is not for the convenience of services. It is simply to serve the hopes, dreams and visions of the focus person. If the focus is on a whole family or on a team of people in an organization, then the aim is to serve the vision of the team. It is very exciting work.

Thus, person-centered planning is a group of methods of action focused on a particular human being or group of human beings (families, organizations) who want to make a design, drawing or map into the future.

The words are straightforward and we are comfortable with practicing an example of "human being focused planning". But with popularization, a term may be overused, abused, get fuzzy and lose its meaning. We hear many things labeled "person-centered planning" that seem to us to have little to do with the common sense of being focused on human beings. That confuses us. We are comfortable if people want to label the tools we use as person-centered, if they really help meet human needs.

Together we're better

Tools like PATH and MAPS are designed to create and work in *shared space*. We are all familiar with the notion of having *private space*, and it's opposite, *managed space*. Much less common is the understanding of *shared space,* the middle ground between these choices.

When MAPS and PATH are attempted in *private space*, they tend to push the boundaries of individualism and isolation into shared space and interdependence. It is in the nature of the tools to challenge a life lived exclusively within private boundaries.

When, PATH and MAPS are attempted in *managed space*, they will (by their nature) tend to challenge the system's boundaries, often beyond comfortable bureaucratic limits. *Managed space* tends to be bureaucratic, requires dependence and obedience to system defined controls. There are places and times when we all need *managed space.* However, anyone who chooses to use person-centered planning to follow the mandate of a managed system should read the warning label: MAPS and PATH are designed to create *shared space*, a space of interdependence in between individualism and total control.

Because systems are designed to create a particular kind of stability, and to counter any challenge to their authority and the perimeters of their turf, when a person-centered plan challenges it's power, the system reacts in defense. This may appears to be out of all proportion to the strength of the probe created by the MAP or PATH, but the response is not to the actual probe. The system reacts to the challenge to its power and authority over people. Knowing this in advance is an important safeguard.

Shared space is an uncommon space, an underdeveloped space, an unknown space, that we believe needs to be nurtured so we can all grow stronger together. Teamwork, collaboration, cooperation, interdependence, sharing, are all difficult concepts to actualize in our society. They are concepts that find their meaning in shared space. Shared space is where we believe in we —not me. We believe we need to create a new emphasis on shared space in our culture, so we can learn to live with one another.

Our core concept: Giftedness

Shared space is the sacred space where gifts and giftedness can be best realized. Giftedness is the core assumption that every person (without exception) has gifts to contribute to society, and that a healthy society will invest the time and energy to listen to and nurture the gifts in every person to be a fully participating citizen.

Gifts are constrained in *private space* because a gift is only a gift when it is given, therefore, in isolation giftedness is limited.

In *managed space*, giftedness is difficult because in systems that highlight zero-sum competition, people do not want to give things away. Where there has to be a loser in order to be a winner, most people want to own, sell, manage, and control. Only certified officials are empowered to give, and only within formal guidelines. Thus, giving of gifts undermines the foundations of control.

Giftedness as a concept innocently challenges managed space at its very roots.

Understanding MAPS and PATH

MAPS and PATH first and foremost are tools to help restore dreams and ignite hope by drawing people together to envision and plan and enact constructive futures. For us, MAPS and PATH are not just another way of doing a service plan, they represent a different way of thinking. They are definitely not more of the same thing.

MAPS and PATH are designed as healing tools for people and for organizations. They are in fact more spiritual than technical, which is one of the reasons they are difficult to bureaucratize. They must be used with skill and heart, a practice rooted in an ethic of 'do no harm'. This is not simply a matter of technique, it is more an art. There are technical competencies to master, but this is not the difficult part. As an art, person-centered planning requires facilitators to be able to truly listen to people's dreams and nightmares. Next, their hopes and visions must be shaped into sustainable images. Finally, there is a translation into practical daily routines that move them safely in the direction of the dream. Facilitation requires giving over control by taking and practicing the power to move from a position of power over others to power with them.

We have invested time and energy in developing MAPS and PATH because we think they make a difference in the lives of real human beings. We believe that these tools are for all of us. We are all human beings. We believe everyone wants and deserves, simply by virtue of being born human, a chance to live fulfilling lives where gifts and capacities are recognized and utilized.

All of us, at various times of our lives, are in situations where we cannot manage alone, our abilities are trapped, and only our 'deficiencies' are noticed. At such times, we need tools to reach out, to renew, to recommission our 'mission', to find the power in our dream, so we can be full, healthy, contributing citizens. That's where MAPS and PATH fit for us.

The answer to when to use MAPS and PATH is, when they are needed. We hear people voicing concerns that MAPS and PATH are being mutilated, mandated, perverted and used incorrectly. It is true, they are. However, the bigger truth is, we have no control over what people do. Thus, our choice is to focus on creating the best tools we can, and providing the most human and thoughtful guidelines and training we can devise in the hope that people using the tools will 'do no harm'.

We choose to focus our energy on the majority of people with talent and good will who are also searching for tools to create new futures and full lives for themselves and for the people they serve. We know that the key problem in the misuse and abuse of tools is not in the design or regulation of the tools, but is in the spirit of the implementers.

People who want to exert power over others will use any tool to enhance their control. The only controls we choose to exert are clear ethical guidelines. Thus, if people with power choose to plan for people without having them present, the label on the tool makes no difference, but simply becomes another deceptive shell game to take or sustain power and control. We believe it is not ethical to plan for a person if the person is excluded.

Pre-conditions for MAPS and PATH

Presence is a precondition, the first layer of ethical implementation. Those with the skills to make things happen, must do what it takes and make sure that the seldom heard voices are heard clearly and in full voice. This means no one ever plans alone. It means someone who has difficulty speaking with words has friends and loved ones with them, to ensure that their voice, their ideas, are heard clearly. It does not mean that every whimsical idea becomes a goal.

In a MAP or a PATH, friends and colleagues struggle together with complex realities and make difficult choices. Good facilitators create a safe space which honors the dreams, nightmares, aspirations and talents of the focus person. There is no guarantee of the good life. There is no magic bullet. MAPS and PATH are simply tools to help someone create and plan their own life.

Listening is the heart of MAPS and PATH. We believe that actually listening to one another is foundation for these tools. Through listening (not rebutting and arguing) we gather the best information and resources we can muster, then we make the best decisions we can. There are no magic wands. There is just the long haul, hard work that all of us must do to realize fully lived lives in these complex and challenging times.

Good facilitators hold empty containers (questions) in front of people, then wait, and listen to the silence. The tension in this silence creates a safe space for people to fill with their deep yearnings and simple unspoken needs, the real stuff of life. As facilitators, we open an inviting, empty space in front of the focus person, and ensure that their ideas and wishes are heard. Hearing does not imply agreement, but simply honest, accurate listening to the message. Then the hard work begins – determining what to do.

Dangers in MAPS and PATH

We wish that by designing good tools, and using them well, we could guarantee a healthy positive future, for us and for others. Unfortunately, there is no such guarantee. What we can say is that if we do **not** plan well and work hard, the incidence of abuse and trauma will be higher. We can tell you from our own experience, that being on the journey, engaging in the struggle for a meaningful life, is the best guarantee anyone can offer. No one can promise that anyone will reach a specific goal, but we can at least guarantee that the journey will be a fascinating one. As Helen Keller said: "Life is a daring adventure, or nothing at all!" Choose life!

MAPS and PATH are healing tools on a spiritual journey. They are not just another chart or meeting. Skilled facilitators know that all of us are at risk. With humility, they endeavor to enhance the strengths and capacities of every focus person. To do this, facilitators must create of a zone of safety. People who cannot create a safe place for a person to unfurl their most delicate and fragile dreams and fears should stay away from this type of work. Hearing peoples dreams and hopes is a sacred trust. Without mutual respect, people will be hurt.

Facilitators can harm people. Shattering dreams is unacceptable. It must not be done! Paradoxically, the art is to balance dreams with doable, positive and possible steps, steps which can and will be implemented by a group of people working together. MAPS and PATH create the links between the dreams we all have (no matter how fragile) and the practical daily steps that begin and sustain us on our life journey. Maps and PATH do not guarantee we will achieve our dreams; they do help us to live our lives on a journey of hope, accomplishment and wonder. On that journey, there will be disappointment, tragedy and frustration. This is why we need tools so we can stay on a path that has the potential to help us realize our dreams.

Commodifying these tools is dangerous. We shudder when people try to commodify MAPS and PATH to meet bureaucratic requirements. Maps and PATH generate the information which can be translated to accommodate bureaucratic requirements (which are a fact of our lives), but the danger is in comodifying the art of these tools rather than translating the results to meet legitimate system requirements. Commodification betrays the people first foundation on which they are constructed.

There are two antidotes to dangerous practices.

Accountability. Critics say that MAPS and PATH are not accountable because they are not primarily responsive to the needs of bureaucratic structures. We disagree. They are profoundly accountable. The stumbling block is, accountable to whom? Person-centered planning tools are accountable to the individual, family or team on whom they are focused. Example, if I have a PATH done with me, the ultimate arbiter of whether it is useful (or not) is not a neatly completed document in a file –it is me! Creative people in systems can translate this real accountability into the type of data required by funders.

Interdependence. Some are concerned that MAPS and PATH are individualistic. A better understanding would say that they are personalized and promote interdependence. Substantial portions of the tools ask us who is in our circle; who do we need to enroll to accompany us through the specific actions it will take over time to make our dream happen? These questions direct us to explore and develop our interdependence rather than our isolation.

Planning and implementation

Do MAPS and PATH always work? No! A good plan is simply a clear direction with a strong foundation for the hope that the people involved will work to make something positive happen. There are no guarantees. When person-centered planning tools are used correctly with the spirit of the heart, they are **never** about a person in isolation and always about a person (or a family or group) in a context of interdependence. The plan mobilizes that network of people to be part of the implementation. The illusion that any person-centered planning tool finished after two hours or a day is a misrepresentation of its essence.

Is there an implementation plan and a way to follow-up? Person-centered planning tools are for changing your life and have implementation included in the process. If there is no implementation plan, then the tool was used inappropriately. The plan is not done because it is posted on the wall, or placed on a chart. It is fulfilled as a person lives it. Judith Snow wisely says, "The first step at the end of a PATH is truly the next step. When will we meet next? Who will we invite? All this must happen soon after the initial planning event. And committed circle members continue that process."

Safeguards for MAPS and PATH

Integrity principle. Do it for yourself first. Perhaps the most significant precaution we can offer is the guideline that no person should use any person-centered planning tool on anyone else until they have lived through the experience personally. That does not mean sitting in a group and observing a PATH, or watching a video. It means having had your own PATH or MAP, or whatever done with you and your family and friends. This takes courage, but people who have done it report that they are better facilitators and listeners. They understand from their heart the incredible vulnerability required for any person to put their hopes and fears out in the open. Therefore, people who have experienced these tools personally are more respectful and are much less likely to do harm. Those who have not experienced these tools personally should **not** use them on other people. It is a matter of respect and safety. The best facilitators walk the talk as much as possible.

Collaboration principle. Never do it alone. Do not facilitate these processes alone because it models the dangerous assumption that we can manage life alone. There is safety in partnership. By the same token, the focus person must never be alone. It isn't safe. And in the rare circumstance that someone is alone, all person-centered planning tools worth their salt will identify and begin to overcome that loneliness immediately. Collaborate; collaborate; collaborate.

Safety principle. Do No Harm. There are times when choosing to do nothing is a discerning decision. Better to be humble and nervous about your capacities than to leap into unknown waters and do irreparable damage. This is **not** an excuse to never take a risk, but rather to be cautious with other people's lives. Respect them. There are even times to stop a process mid-stream. Do no harm! Take risks, but choose the time, the place, and a tool that give an excellent chance of success. That is all any of us can do.

Self-reflection and review. We must constantly reflect and review what and how we are doing with these tools. Just because we have learned the process does not mean we are doing our best. There is always room for improvement. Maybe we are over-tired, or perhaps we are not the right people to undertake a particular MAP. We must listen to these itchy patches and pay attention. Self-reflection and review are a process of constant improvement ; our learning and relearning is always a work in progress.

The facilitator: Paradox in action

Good facilitators struggle to balance many seemingly paradoxical issues.

Learning *and* unlearning. Facilitators must constantly learn new things, and unlearn some old ones. The facilitator is a servant to both the person and the process. The facilitator basically holds empty containers and draws the content from the person and his/her friends, family and colleagues. The plan belongs to the person not the organization or the facilitator. We must learn to hand over power and unlearn our control habits.

Knowledge *and* self-knowledge. One must have a wide knowledge base, and a strong knowing sense of self. As a facilitator one must give up preconceived notions of what is good or bad, what is possible or impossible. This requires knowing yourself, your strengths and your limits in order to distinguish between personal preferences and those of the person we are serving. The facilitator is not passive but rather pushy in getting the content from the person. This takes practice because we too often stand in judgment and thus block the PATH or MAP from truly belonging to the focus person. Dangerous facilitators override another person's words and images with their own interpretations.

Professional *and* personal integrity. There is no separation between personal and professional integrity. Integrity is integrity.

Separate ethics creates schizophrenia and harms people. To minimize this risk, our ethics rule is that facilitators must practice these tools on their own lives before using them on others. This makes us more respectful and less dangerous.

Can everyone facilitate MAPS and PATH? That is like asking if everyone can do brain surgery. Opening people's hearts and dreams is surgery on the soul. It is delicate work and must be honored with skill, compassion and love. It is also hard work. In exploring your skill set, if you discover this is not your strength, listen to yourself and, without beating up on yourself, find others with the gifts to do this work. We have seen magic happen when MAPS and PATH are used with skill, love, imagination and humility.

Beware. We feel it is unfair at best and obscene at worst to ask others to dream and to be vulnerable, while we remain aloof –hiding behind the mask of so called professionalism. A brilliant professional is one who has explored the depths of her own soul and who knows the boundaries necessary to allow others to share their pain and joy without intruding or invading that space. We tell people, "Beware of facilitators who advise you what to do, but whose own lives are a gigantic mess and who can't ask for help themselves."

For us, the heart of person-centered planning is, "Facilitator, know thyself". This is no mean feat in a culture that spends billions to convince us all to think it is cool to be young, white, bright, straight and thin.

Personal check list for good facilitation

Good facilitators are basically good listeners who see their role as creatively helping people design their lives at they desire. That's what person-centered planning is really all about.

Here are a few guiding questions for facilitators to ask themselves:

- Have you yourself experienced being the focus of a MAP or a PATH?
- Do you have a mentor, guide, therapist, circle you see regularly to check out your own life?
- Do you read and study continuously in group dynamics, organizational change, healing, health, etc.? Do you read outside your own field to increase your scope?
- Do you think you have been trained and certified because you took a three day course on MAPS or PATH? If so, return to the first point.

- Do you alphabetize processes into acronyms like "PCP"? Please don't. The initialized version trivializes a deep issue. We don't want people reporting that they were PCP'd upon.
- Do you work alone, or do you have partners with whom to share experiences and reflect on your learning?

Using MAPS and PATH

Which people? MAPS and PATH are for all people. They are not about disability. They are about focusing on human beings to help design and develop plans for their future. If we see people as clients or consumers, or if we assert power over people, we are not doing MAPS or PATH. These tools are for interdependent human beings, not clients or consumers. This is full of paradox because it is simultaneously a very simple concept and enormously difficult to implement. It requires us to challenge and refocus values that we learned wrong and must relearn. This is hard but necessary work.

Creative links. The artist, the architect, the musician, the poet, the writer all have much to teach us about person-centered planning. We see this human centered approach incorporating the passion, commitment and courage of the arts. Person-centered planning is about uncovering what is already there, what is deep within each and every one of us. A sculptor sees a piece of art in the raw stone or wood. An architect envisions a building when overseeing a naked piece of earth. A musician hears a score in the breeze and in her head. So too the artist of person-centered planning sees the full human being through the layers of societal rules and norms, which have often corroded and encased the human spirit.

It is the job of the facilitator to be like the architect or sculptor who uncovers the person already there, with a soul yearning to be whatever her gifts reveal. Society teaches us well to "cover up" our realness. Too often, we turn to find our true selves only when we are on the verge of collapse, depression or addiction.

Nourishing human growth. People with disabilities have often been buried under a ton of labels and phrases that mask who they are. The more oppressed and vulnerable the human being the more talented and sensitive the artist facilitator needs to be. We know from research on health that there are universal needs to meet as people help one another to grow into human beings. People need food and shelter, to love and to be loved, to have friends and to belong, and to discover and create a meaningful life.

In working to uncover the person hiding behind the mask of fear, insecurity and anxiety, the facilitator must be a person who has dealt with life herself. A person who is not afraid of facing whatsoever emerges from another person's heart.

Person-centered planning is, in essence, listening and sharing vulnerability. It is about sharing life, sharing power, giving up control, encouraging interdependence, and getting to what really matters to makes someone's life not perfect, but meaningful. It is about nourishing the humanity and gifts in every one of us.

Can this be done? Yes. Is it easy? No.

Let's see person-centered planning as art. Let's give it the color, passion, power, emotion, magic, skill and talent it deserves.

Let's start with a blank sheet of paper as our metaphor, a sheet radiant with the patient capacity to record any dream. Let's assist people in creating and designing their own beautiful futures. Let's work together to do this as we become warriors for peace. Peace and justice will not come by us wishing it. It will come with the blood, sweat and tears that real change always entails. Let's join together to build a new society. Let's start in our own backyards with our own friends and networks of support.

It really comes down to very simple things that require our life long commitment...

> *"Piglet sidled up to Pooh from behind.*
> *'Pooh!' he whispered.*
> *'Yes, Piglet?'*
> *'Nothing,' said Piglet, taking Pooh's paw. 'I just wanted to be sure of you.'*
> *" I will not drag you along; I will not leave you alone; I will stand by you and have my hand there for you to hold when you need to."*
>
> *– Winnie the Pooh*

14

Telling New Stories
The Search for Capacity

John O'Brien & Beth Mount

> *Some stories enhance life;*
> *others degrade it.*
> *So we must be careful*
> *about the stories we tell,*
> *about the ways we define*
> *ourselves and other people.*
> —*Burton Blatt*

Consider these two stories:

I

Mr. Davis has a mental age of 3 years, 2 months. IQ = 18.
Severe impairment of adaptive behavior, severe range of
mental retardation. Becomes agitated and out of control.
Takes [medicines] for psychosis.

Severely limited verbal ability; inability to comprehend
abstract concepts. Learns through imitation. Has learned
to unlock the Coke machine and restock it, and to crank a
power mower and operate it.

His family is uncooperative. They break appointments and
do not follow through on behavior management plans.

II

Ed lives with his mother and sister in [housing project].
Ten of his relatives live near by and they visit back and
forth frequently. His father spends little time with him, but
two of his sisters have been very helpful when there are
crises. His family agree that he will live with one or an-
other of them for the rest of his life.

Ed is at home in his neighborhood. He visits extended
family members and neighbors daily. He goes to local stores
with his sisters and helps with shopping. He goes to church.
Ed dresses neatly, is usually friendly, and shakes hands with
people when he meets them. He is a very big man, with

*limited ability to speak. When he gets frustrated and upset
he cusses and "talks" to himself in a loud voice. These
characteristics often frighten other people who do not know
him well. He has been excluded from the work activity
center because he acts "out of control" there. He has broken
some furniture and punched holes in the walls there and
scares some of the staff people very much.*

*Ed likes people and enjoys visiting in the neighborhood. He
loves music, dancing, and sweeping. He likes loading
vending machines and operating mechanical equipment.
He likes to go shopping. He likes to cook for himself and for
other people and can fix several meals on the stove at home.
He likes to hang clothes and bring them in off the line. He
likes to stack cord wood and help people move furniture.
He prefers tasks that require strength and a lot of large
muscle movement.*

Both of these stories were told to help the same man. But they differ in the way they were constructed, in their purpose, in their consequences, and in the assumptions they shape about human development and human service organization. The group that constructed the first story speaks a different language from the group that enacted the second story.

Different rules for construction

An interdisciplinary team told the first story in its required annual review of Mr. Davis' progress. They integrated data from psychological, social work, nursing, speech therapy, and occupational therapy assessments with data about Mr. Davis' performance in the day program. They determined objectives for the next year, recommended additional therapy services, and made a placement recommendation. The team was uncertain about the extent to which Mr. Davis' behavior problems are an expression of psychotic illness and agreed to seek a psychiatric evaluation to settle the question. Mr. Davis was not at the meeting because he had acted out violently that day, and staff had sent him home to his mother in compliance with the team's behavior management plan. Though the social worker sent an invitation, no one from his family attended. The meeting took twenty minutes.

A group of people who know and care about Mr. Davis and his family told the second story as part of a collective search for a better response to his situation. An outside facilitator, conducting research for her doctoral dissertation (Mount, 1987), met Mr. Davis and his family at the suggestion of the day program director. With his mother and sister and two direct service workers, the facilitator organized a personal futures planning group. Staff people from the day program joined Mr. Davis, members of his extended family, neighbors, and church members at the family's church on a Sunday afternoon. They told stories about Mr. Davis and his family, expressed their concerns for his situation and their ideas about his future, shared information about opportunities in the neighborhood, and came up with suggested next steps. Several people, including program staff, took personal responsibility for action steps and agreed to meet again to review progress, without the facilitator. The facilitator recorded the meeting on large posters, using color coded graphic symbols and quotations from participants. Mr Davis sat with one of his sisters during the meeting. He asked for, and carried home, the poster that described the group's ideas about his future. The first meeting took two hours.

Different purposes

Professionals told the first story in compliance with state regulations in order to control the routine work of direct service staff. Their story justifies Mr Davis' eligibility for the program and the program's responses to his problem behaviors. It takes existing service arrangements as a given.

People who know Mr Davis and his family told the second story voluntarily in order to discover actions that will reveal capacities in him, in the people who care about him, and in his neighborhood. Their story justifies action to expand his opportunities and learn better ways to support him. It calls for changes in existing service arrangements from the time and place of planning meetings to the mission and activities of the day program.

The people who told the first story selected objectives for Mr. Davis which would increase his time on task at the assembly contract the center works on, increase his accuracy in performing a letter folding simulation to improve his small motor coordination, and ready him to prepare meals by identifying menu items from pictures of the four food groups. Noting an increase in his problem behavior, they recommended his admission to a psychiatric hospital for evaluation and mental health treatment. Noting his unmet need for speech therapy and his mother's difficulty in following through on required programs, they recommended post-psychiatric hospital placement in the regional mental retardation institution for intensive training. While the plan arising from their meeting was being typed, Mr. Davis was excluded from the program in response to staff concern for their safety and the safety of other clients.

The people who told the second story responded to their account of Mr. Davis' preferences and neighborhood resources to deal with the idleness resulting from his exclusion from the day program and the threat of institutionalization. They decided that he preferred hard physical work and work with machines to sedentary tasks requiring fine movements. Within three days, one of his sisters and a direct service staff person had developed an opportunity for him to load soft drink vending machines at three convenience stores in his neighborhood. Within two weeks another sister and a neighbor had begun to create a schedule of lawn mowing, fire wood stacking, and yard work that he and one of his cousin's could share, with occasional assistance from a center staff person. They recognized his ability to help out at home and encouraged his mother to increase her expectations of regular and reliable performance. They acknowledged that he was a welcome visitor in many neighborhood homes and shared what they had learned about how to understand his communication and deal with his occasional episodes of talking to himself and blowing off steam. They agreed that there was no reason for Mr. Davis to go to the psychiatric hospital or the mental retardation institution.

Different consequences

The tellers of the second story did not aim for perfection, nor have they achieved it. Three years after this process began, Mr. Davis still loads machines and does outside work daily, but these activities do not add up to a full time job and he receives very little cash for his efforts. He remains active and helpful around his house and among his neighbors. He has had no help to improve his ability to communicate, though there have been several unproductive referrals. He continues to talk to himself but has not had a frightening episode in more than a year. A number of the people who gathered at the first meeting still meet regularly to share what they are doing and learning about Mr. Davis and what they might do together next.

Think for a moment about organizations as systems for interpreting their own actions and their environments (Daft & Weick, 1986): as a set of processes for telling stories about...

... what has happened in and around the organization

... what events mean to organization members

... what to do next

Assmptions about effective organization and human development shape, and in turn are shaped by, the ways human service organizations make sense of their world.

Different assumptions –> Different organizations

The first story assumes that professional people who share very little of Mr. Davis' daily life can speak the most important words about him. These words have power because they are objective data, the (often quantitative) results of scientific procedures. Things will be better for Mr Davis if he, his family, and direct service workers, non-experts all, listen to and obey professional plans. The second story assumes that Mr Davis himself, and those who share and shape his daily life, should be the primary speakers. Knowledge and the power to effectively bind action arise primarily from personal commitment, careful listening, and shared action. When available technology is insufficient to cure, the role of experts is to listen and cooperate.

The first story assumes that Mr. Davis remains the same person no matter where and how you meet him. What needs to be known about him is disclosed by viewing him in isolation from his social context (Sarason, 1981). His measured intelligence fixes his potential for development unequivocally and dictates his future (Gould, 1981). The second story assumes that Mr. Davis' life can only be understood in context. He is both unable to meet the prerequisites for cooking and able to fix meals. He is both dangerous and friendly. He is both "that big crazy boy" and a welcome guest in some people's homes. He is both unable to speak and a dancer. His potential for development is the product of his efforts and the efforts of his allies and assistants (Bronfenbrenner, 1977). He can only be revealed when people join with him to create his future. In this sense his potential is unknown and unknowable apart from action that he and the others he relies on decide to take together.

The first story assumes that Mr. Davis will be helped if the tellers exhaustively catalog his deficiencies. Their conversation is dominated by what he can't do, what he won't do, and why he doesn't. The second story assumes that capacity, interest, and preference make the foundation of effective help. What he likes, what he wants to do, and his vocation among us centers storytelling and action.

The first story assumes that human services exist to change Mr. Davis. Accurate classification leads to appropriate placement and good diagnosis leads to proper prescription. If Mr. Davis complies with the prescribed program, he will progress as far as he is able (Biklen, 1988). Services change by learning to do what they are doing better. The second story assumes that human services exist to assist Mr. Davis by supporting him, his family, and friends to develop and pursue community opportunities (O'Brien & Lyle, 1989). Services develop by learning to do new things in new ways (Argyris & Schon, 1978).

The first story assumes that reliable and effective service results from hierarchical structures controlled by rational argument among experts who find pre-existing answers by standard examination (Weick & Browning, 1986). Impersonal statements, standardized scores, quantified objectives, linear logic, and appeals to authority shape the organization. The second story assumes that reliable and effective service results from collaboration across organizational boundaries influenced by shared visions and shaped by negotiation of multiple differences. Answers don't preexist, they are constructed by the way people organize to find them (Maturana & Varela, 1980) and communicated in the narratives people share (Weick, 1987). Personal testimony, graphic images, shared food, music, laughter and tears, and creative action shape the organization.

Raymond Kilroy, a wise and vigorous advocate for himself and other people with disabilities, gave testimony to the US Senate about his vision for himself and all people with disabilities (Kilroy, 1987). His vision compels attention to new directions for all of us.

> *We are moving away from emphasizing my needs toward building upon my capacities. We are moving away from providing services to me in some facility toward building bridges with me to communities and neighborhood associations. We are moving away from programing me and other people with disabilities toward empowering us and our families to acquire the support we want. We are moving away from focusing on my deficits to focusing on my competence. We are moving away from specialized disability*

> *organizations so that we can develop and sustain relation-*
> *ships with people who will depend upon people like me*
> *and upon whom people like me can depend.*

To move toward this future we must all learn to listen to, to tell, and to act on new stories, stories whose theme is action to discover capacity.

References

Argyris, C. & Schon, D. (1978). *Organizational learning: A* theory of action perspective. Reading, MA: Addison-Wesley.

Biklen, D. (1988). The myth of clinical judgement. *Journal of Social Issues, 44* (1), 127-140.

Blatt, B. (1987). *The conquest of mental retardation.* Austin, TX: Pro-Ed.

Bronfenbrenner, U. (1977). Toward an experimental ecology of human development. *American Psychologist, 32,* 513-531.

Daft, R. & Weick, K. (1984). Toward a model of organizations as interpretation systems. *Academy of Management Review, 9* (2), 284-295.

Gould, S. (1981). *The mismeasure of man.* New York: Norton.

Kilroy, R. (1987). Testimony to the United States Senate Sub-committee on the Labor & Human Resources, April 23.

Maturana, H. & Varela, F. (1980) *Autopoiesis and cognition.* Boston: Reidel.

Mount, B. (1987). *Personal futures planning: Finding directions for change* (Doctoral dissertation, University of Georgia). Dissertation Abstracts International. (University Microfilms No-87-24642).

O'Brien, J. (1987). A guide to personal futures planning. In B. Wilcox & G. T Bellamy (Eds.), *A comprehensive guide to the activities catalog.* Baltimore: Paul Brookes.

O'Brien, J. & Lyle, C. (1989). *Framework for accomplishment.* Lithonia, GA: Responsive Systems Associates.

Weick, K. (1987). Organizational culture as a source of high reliability. *California Management Review, 29* (2), 112-127.

Weick, K. & Browning, L. (1986). Argument and narration in organizational communication. *Journal of Management, 12* (2), 243-259.

15

Finding A Way Toward Everyday Lives
The Contribution of Person-centered Planning

John O'Brien & Herbert Lovett[*]

Person-centered Planning can
invite, align, & direct
shared efforts to create...

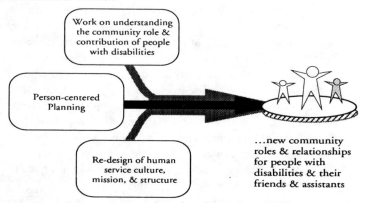

Work on understanding
the community role &
contribution of people
with disabilities

Person-centered
Planning

...new community
roles & relationships
for people with
disabilities & their
friends & assistants

Re-design of human
service culture,
mission, & structure

Foundations of person-centered planning

The term, person-centered planning, refers to a family of approaches to organizing and guiding community change in alliance with people with disabilities and their families and friends.

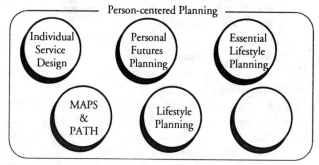

Person-centered Planning

Individual
Service
Design

Personal
Futures
Planning

Essential
Lifestyle
Planning

MAPS
&
PATH

Lifestyle
Planning

[*] On 29–30 June 1992, the PENNSYLVANIA DEPARTMENT OF PUBLIC WELFARE, OFFICE OF MENTAL RETARDATION sponsored a conference that gathered people experienced in various approaches to person-centered planning and advocates and administrators interested in learning more about person-centered planning. The conference, which was coordinated by Pennsylvania Association of Resources for People with Mental Retardation (PAR), provided background information for this booklet.

Each approach to person-centered planning has distinctive practices, but all share a common foundation of beliefs:

- The person at the focus of planning, and those who love the person, are the primary authorities on the person's life direction. The essential questions are, *Who is this person?* and *What community opportunities will enable this person to pursue his or her interests in a positive way?*

  - Knowledge gained from close, respectful, continuing relationships with the focus person is crucial in answering these questions.

  - Information gained from technical assessments of the person can be helpful, but only in the context of a knowledgeable account of a person's history and desired future. Subordinating professional-technical information to personal knowledge turns the typical agency decision making process on its head.

- The purpose of person-centered planning is learning through shared action. People who engage in person-centered planning may produce documentation of their meetings, proposals, contract specifications, or budgets. These are only footprints: the path is made by people walking together.

  - The focus person and those who know the person best may be uncertain about what is possible or desirable for the person. One function of person-centered planning is to decrease such uncertainty by encouraging people to try new things together and to learn from them.

  - The focus person and others the focus person relies on may disagree about what is possible or desirable for the person. Disagreements may be explicit and verbal or they may surface in the behavior of all of the people involved. One function of person-centered planning is to provide a forum for negotiating such conflicts.

- Person-centered planning aims to change common patterns of community life. Segregation and congregation of people with disabilities are common. Devaluing stereotypes and inappropriately low expectations are common. Denial of opportunity is common. These negative patterns do not necessarily signify mean-spiritedness so much as undesirable habit. If invited to assist a person to pursue a desirable future, some people may remain closed and rejecting, but others will respond generously, based on their sense of justice. Person-centered planning stimulates community hospitality and enlists community members in assisting focus people to define and to work toward a desirable future.

- In order to support the kinds of community changes necessary to improve people's chances for a desirable future, virtually all existing human service policies and agencies will have to change the ways they regard people, the ways they relate to communities, the ways they spend money, the ways they define staff roles and responsibilities, and the ways they exercise authority. Person-centered planning requires collaborative action and fundamentally challenges practices that separate people and perpetuate controlling relationships.

- Honest person-centered planning can only come from respect for the dignity and completeness of the focus person. This respect leads those involved in person-centered planning to work for...
  ... equal, non-coercive relationships with the people they plan with
  ... appreciation and celebration of each person's uniqueness, and constructive ways to understand one another's challenges and failings
  ... effective ways to communicate the importance of respect and equality to others involved with the focus person.

- Assisting people to define and pursue a desirable future tests one's clarity, commitment, and courage. Person-centered planning engages powerful emotional and ethical issues and calls for sustained search for effective ways to deal with difficult barriers and conflicting demands. Those who treat person-centered planning simply as a technique and those who fail to provide for their own development and support will offer little benefit to the people they plan with.

How does person-centered planning influence change?
Person-centered planning influences change by...
... creating a compelling image of a desirable future and inviting people to join with the focus person to make it happen
... strengthening personal relationships
... helping people plan, act, and learn by reflecting on their successes and failures

When successful, person-centered planning allows its participants to experience tension between what is desirable for a person and what exists now for the person. This tension can energize action for positive change.

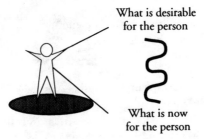

Too often, however, the inertia of service systems couples with prejudice against people with disabilities to stifle hope and opportunity. For change to happen, community opportunities must be opened and expanded and service systems must develop new capacities, both within themselves and in the wider communities of which they must be a part.

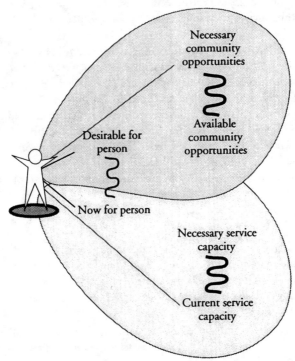

This development happens through a process of mutual adaptation: first, services change to create new supports for the person and then the person responds to the demands and the rewards of the new situation. This sequence contradicts the tradition that people with disabilities must change themselves as a condition of entry to new opportunities: environments effect change more powerfully than training can.

Person-centered planning influences change when people respond to the tension between what a community has to offer now and what the focus person needs to pursue a desirable future. Direct engagement with the focus person and the focus person's allies· guides community development. Person-centered planning is a source of clear invitations to community members.

Person-centered planning frequently challenges the culture of most human service agencies. Despite many capable staff who care about what happens to the people they serve, service system culture typically values uniformity and predictability more than the needs of any single individual.

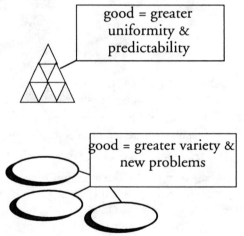

Person-centered planning primarily values accurate individual services. This greatly increases the required variety of service responses.

When uniformity and predictability are primary system values, "individual program planning" functions to decrease uncertainty and variety through a regulated, impersonal ("objective") process of judgement that specifies people's daily routines in the pre-existing service option that best matches their disabling condition. The purpose and effect of individual program planning is to make the system more stable by drawing clear boundaries between staff and client and by teaching staff and families and people with disabilities a way to think about people's needs that matches the system's routines.

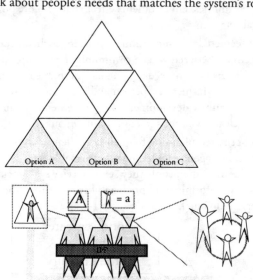

Individual Program Planning: Reduces system uncertainty by complying with rules governing...
  • Measuring the person

  • Assigning the person to an available option

  • Prescribing & monitoring treatment

We have historically been more efficient in providing people for services than services for people. Person-centered planning reverses this tradition to create a personalized image of a desirable future and a problem solving process for moving toward that future. In effect, effective person-centered planning de-stabilizes a system for individualized schedules and types of assistance. The questions of how best to understand this person and how best to refine this understanding in action are central to the process instead of being the givens of regulations and professional training. Boundaries between professional and client are dissolved in the search for equal, non-coercive relationships. Boundaries between service agency and community are re-drawn as people seek to develop new opportunities. While some people will find these yet-to-be charted areas of work exciting, others, understandably, will find this unsettling and threatening.

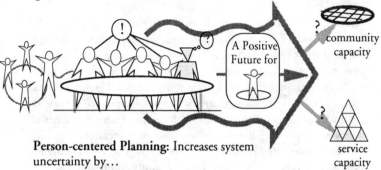

Person-centered Planning: Increases system uncertainty by…
- Strengthening the person's alliances
- Clarifying individual interests & needs
- Energizing new demands on system & community

Those who want to can find many ways to avoid engaging the tension between current reality and a desirable personal future. They can compare the present to worse past conditions instead of comparing it to desirable future capacities. They can dismiss the image of a desirable future as unrealistic. They can say that they would like to help but that powerful outside forces forbid them. They can stay busy with activities that allow no time to listen to and learn from focus people.

Individual, community, and service development all happen through a learning process which builds on existing capacities and searches for ways to deal constructively with obstacles. Capacities and obstacles come from local relationships among people with disabilities, families, community members, and service agencies as much or more than they are imposed by uncontrollable outside forces. Person-centered planning provides a systematic way to learn from sustained action over the months and years necessary for development. If the process is successful, people's sense of a desirable future will evolve. One of the most common misunderstandings of person-centered planning is that it is a short series of meetings whose purpose is to produce a static plan. This misunderstanding leads people to underestimate the time, effort, uncertainty, anxiety and surprise necessary to accurately support people's lives over time.

Limitations of person-centered planning

Done competently, person-centered planning focuses and directs the energy available to the focus person. Each effort uniquely contends with limits on effective action by the focus person and the focus person's allies.

Sometimes limitations come from the service system. Many administrators like to talk about paradigm shifts without investing in the hard work required to make basic change in the way an agency operates. At times one agency or part of an agency will want to make more change than the system that contains it wants to accommodate. Substantive change cannot happen when service workers are unclear in their commitment to change, and administrators offer lukewarm support. Some service systems are so incoherent or inert that person-centered planning contributes to good results only for people with very energetic and creative family and friends.

Sometimes limitations come from the focus person.

- The focus person provides some of the energy necessary for change.
  - Some people's interests and gifts are clear to others and so their ideas about a desirable future offer others definite ways to be involved; others' interests and gifts are more difficult to discern or support. Experience shows that people's apparent level of ability does not relate to the clarity with which they can communicate their interests or enlist other people they know to assist them. However, person-centered planning will usually move more slowly and have a narrower reach when a focus person's interests are not clear. It has also been our invariable experience that people's interests are unclear until they have people in their lives who combine their love with optimism.
  - Some focus people welcome other people into their lives; others challenge those who would establish a relationship, sometimes because they have been repeatedly abandoned or abused. Many people with a reputation for being very challenging respond well to the attitudes implicit in person-centered planning, but person-centered planning often requires hard work to establish, and maintain, relationships when the focus person has a difficult or painful history of relating to others. Person-centered planning is not a remedy

for people who are difficult to serve, but it can guide dysfunctional services to provide better contexts for people's growth.

- The focus person's family can make an important contribution, and person-centered planning often provides an effective vehicle for families to have the kind of influence they wish.
  - Family members often have connections to community life and can invite their friends to become involved.
  - Family members often hold the stories that define the focus person as a person rather than a "client". Where services often lose a person's history, or narrowly understand it in terms of professional assessments, families can hold the person's individuality in the foreground of discussions. But family members can lose touch with a focus person, sometimes because of service practices that discourage family involvement.

- Family members and professionals alike can define people in clinical terms.
  - Both family members and professionals can have more influence over than involvement in a person's life. Sometimes professionals have advised family members not to get "over-involved". Similarly, professionals with the most power in people's lives often do not have much direct contact with them. Psychologists may write influential assessments on the basis of very brief encounters, and administrators can make life defining decisions based on service expediency rather than a compelling sense of the person's identity and needs
  - This atmosphere of remote control casts people in a negative light. This focuses planning on people's perceived deficits rather than their capacities; on what could go wrong rather than on what people need for things to go right. When power holders —whether professionals or family members— persist in seeing people in discouraging ways, desirable personal futures become difficult to achieve indeed.

Some limitations on person-centered planning come from the amount of learning necessary to create the opportunities and supports a person needs. Even with strong leadership from the focus person and family and commitment to change by service providers, some issues —such as helping people to make friends, or discovering positive daytime roles for people with high needs for assistance, or finding a constructive way to deal with offenses against the law— are complex and require commitment to the person, often over years.

Person-centered planning is not a "quick fix" for people's difficulties. And, when things do work well, the lessons don't necessarily generalize widely. What seems to be one person's dream could easily be another's nightmare. In this sense, person-centered planning accurately reflects ordinary life.

Some limitations come from the time it takes for things to happen. One focus person's dream, for example, was to live in a housing co-operative, but organizing the cooperative took several years.

These limitations make responsible faciliators of person-centered planning careful not to promise good outcomes from every effort or speedy delivery of personal or organizational change. Responsible policy makers and administrators act cautiously and deliberately when they adopt person-centered planning as a means to attain agency objectives on bureaucratic timeliness.

Controversies among people engaged in person-centered planning

Like any effort that attracts people with a strong desire to contribute to positive social change, person-centered planning has its share of controversies. These debates cut across the different approaches and identify critical areas for the development of person-centered planning.

- Involved people differ about the extent to which the focus person should control the direction of the process. Some people, emphasizing the history of services dominating people's lives "for their own good", want the process only to respond to what the focus person clearly communicates that he or she wants. They say that the process should be "person driven planning", with the focus person unequivocally in the driver's seat. Others, emphasizing the history of services depriving people of opportunities for experiences and relationships, believe that other people must actively invite the focus person into new experiences and new relationships.

- Some people who facilitate person-centered planning would refuse to assist a person who clearly chooses to seek to live in a congregate, disability segregated setting. Others believe that alliance with the person is primary and believe that the process should serve whatever choice of living and daytime arrangements focus people or their families make.

- People who facilitate person-centered planning differ in the amount and kind of information they use. Some choose to enlist the focus person and others in making a broad profile of the person's history, present experiences, and ideas about desirable futures. Others focus on a particular facet of a person's life, such as the necessary and desirable specifications for a person's next living arrangement.

- Some people who facilitate person-centered planning are deeply concerned about working within organized service settings. They believe that service systems will inevitably pervert the possibilities of person-centered planning and choose to work at the very edge of the service system, encouraging people to get out of, or avoid moving into, the system. Others believe that person-centered planning can contribute to reforming services by stimulating, or even requiring, different kinds of service practices. They encourage adaptation of person-centered approaches to fit service system agendas like deinstitutionalization or development of new programs.

- Some people who facilitate person-centered planning believe that person-centered planning should focus on those people who now get the least service from the system: those living with family members. They see person-centered planning as a powerful support to families with disabled members at home and believe that focusing person-centered planning on people already in some kind of residential service is another case of ignoring the many people who have only a little share of system resources in favor of the relatively few in high cost, high visibility services. Others believe that person-centered planning is a particularly effective way to develop better alternatives for people in costly but restrictive and segregating settings.

- People who facilitate person-centered planning disagree about how much a person's family, friends, neighbors, and co-workers or fellow students can do and should be expected to do. Some believe that natural supports (i.e. unpaid people) should and can be sufficient to assist people and that their contribution is blocked by the presence of human service workers. Others believe that, while natural supports make a vital and irreplacable contribution, paid help is necessary and desirable. Still others are uncertain about whether unpaid people will respond on a sustained basis.

- People who facilitate person-centered planning differ about the importance of convening an identified, ongoing support group for the focus person. Some see person-centered planning as a means to the formation of a circle of support and believe that the circle matters much more than the planning process. Others believe that requiring a defined circle of support is somewhat contrived and could deprive some people who are isolated of the benefits that can come from a good plan. Some debate whether paid service providers can be full, effective members of support circles.

A common fear: The debasement of person-centered planning

Regardless of these controversies, most people who facilitate person-centered planning worry that a system more interested in fads than in fundamental change will capture person-centered planning.

Rather than take on the hard work of learning new ways to assist people, service providers can more easily adopt the vocabulary and some of the techniques of person-centered planning. Often this process is not conscious: service providers simply assume that their current beliefs and practices exhaust all of the positive possibilities for the people they serve. It is not so much that they hear people's call for basic change and reject it, as that they listen to people in a way that confirms the rightness of what the system is doing now.

Some signs that person-centered planning has become a system fad rather than a tool for change include:

- System boundaries remain intact. Most of the participants in person-centered planning are system workers. There are few efforts to engage community members. There is little re-allocation of agency resources into community settings.
- Large numbers of people "get" person-centered plans, but there is little work on creating new kinds of relationships, new service

approaches, and new community opportunities. Often this is justified as fairness because administrators believe it would be inequitable to provide something new for a few of the people they serve. This assumes that the system actually has the capacity to respond to everyone's needs. Otherwise, everyone gets a brightly colored bit of paper that describes a future that no one can assist them to pursue.

- The system gives people plans and meetings instead of necessary cash or needed paid for assistance.
- Most talk about person-centered planning focuses on how to improve facilitation of planning meetings rather than on how to change the agency's culture and strategy for investing in community opportunities.
- Administrators require person-centered planning without committing any flexible resources and without a procedure for changing regulations and timelines that create real barriers to necessary changes.
- Administrators, rather than the people involved, tinker with the procedures for person-centered planning in order to make it more efficient and more uniform. For example, administrators decide that person-centered plans take too long and must therefore be completed in a fixed amount of time.
- There is limited investment of time for reflection on what people are learning from person-centered planning.
- Person-centered planning is expected to produce "good stories" more than criticisms and questions about the culture and policies of the service system.

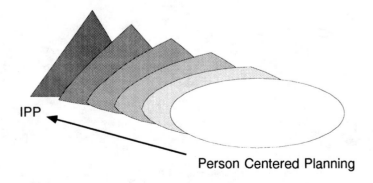

IPP

Person Centered Planning

Person-centered planning can also be defeated by it's enthusiasts. Practitioners can paralyze themselves by agonizing over the problems and ambiguities surfaced in the process instead of looking for small positive steps. Practitioners can disempower themselves by looking for high ground from which to observe and criticize rather than looking for common grounds for action.

These are some possible safeguards which can be initiated by anyone who implements person-centered planning.

- Start small and grow slowly, perhaps with projects that are specifically resourced as development activities.
- Join and invest in building up a network of facilitators and other involved people who can offer mutual support and criticism. The network will grow as people ask for and give one another help.
- Identify and discuss conflicts, uncertainties, and poor outcomes.
- Take advantage of opportunities to learn such as reading and training related to human service values and group leadership.
- Seek advisors and mentors.

Some distinctions between approaches to person-centered planning

From a common foundation of beliefs, each approach to person-centered planning builds a distinctive structure to assist people with disabilities and their allies to clarify direction and plan action.

Individual Service Design

Individual service design developed as part of a long-term effort to assist service providers to understand the practical implications of the principle of normalization (social role valorization). It is often used to help service providers develop positive approaches to people who challenge their ability. The process builds understanding of, and identification with, the focus person by carefully reconstructing the focus person's history. The individual service design group attempts to "walk in the person's shoes", empathically asking what it would it be like to experience the events in the person's life. On the basis of key themes derived from reconstructing the focus person's history, the group identifies the person's most important needs and specifies what would be necessary to meet these needs.

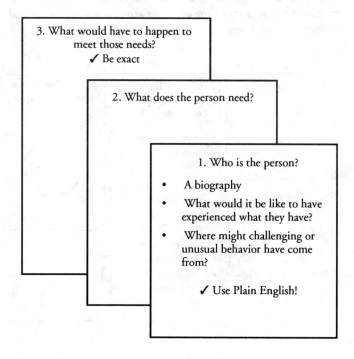

3. What would have to happen to meet those needs?
   ✓ Be exact

2. What does the person need?

1. Who is the person?
   - A biography
   - What would it be like to have experienced what they have?
   - Where might challenging or unusual behavior have come from?

   ✓ Use Plain English!

Personal Futures Planning

Personal futures planning developed from efforts to apply some lessons from the fields of planning and community development to the situation of people with disabilities. Personal futures planning has evolved in two different contexts: support to people with disabilities and their families and friends who begin work with little effective cooperation from the service system; and, assistance to service providers who want to transform the system they work within. The process engages its participants in…

…seeking capacities in the focus person, among those who care about the focus person, and in the focus person's community

…discovering a vision of a desirable future with the focus person and making an action plan

…building stronger and more effective support for the person by joining people in a process of learning through making small positive changes

…specifying and working for changes in the service system which would allow the system to offer more relevant assistance

Personal futures planning calls on all of its participants to work creatively together over time as equals across usual organizational and status boundaries.

1. Finding capacities

Convene the action planning group

Construct a personal profile

- Personal history
- Relationships
- Places
- Choices
- What works/ doesn't
- Ideas about the future

2. Discovering a vision & a plan together

- Review the profile
- Review environmental trends
- Create images of a desirable future
- Identify obstacles & opportunities
- Design strategies
- Commit to next steps
- Identify needed systems changes

3. Building a circle through action

try
fix   reflect

4. Working for systems change

MAPS

MAPS developed from efforts to assist families to include their children with disabilities in ordinary school classrooms. The process brings together students, school staff, and family members to create a shared understanding of the focus person and to clearly identify the focus persons gifts and needs. Based on this shared understanding, participants negotiate modifications to school, family, and individual routines. The MAPS process is closely linked to the creation and development of circles of support for the focus person and often for the family and sometimes for the staff involved. Circles do the day-to day problem solving necessary to make and sustain change.

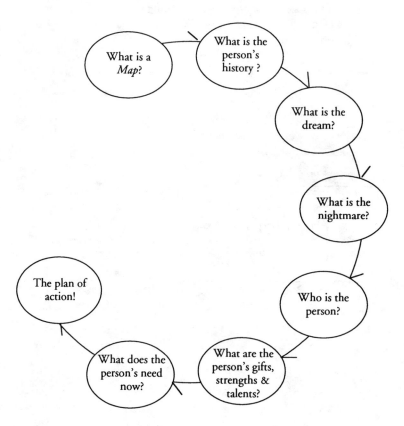

PATH

PATH is a systematic seven step process to define strategies for aligning and increasing the energy available to make progress on complex problems, Complex problems are created whenever people want to serve one another in making socially important purposes real. It is a way for a person and members of their support circle to affirm the values that guide them; vividly depict their vision; feel the tension between their vision and their current reality; identify the people to enroll in making progress; specify the ways they will build the skills, knowledge and stamina necessary for the work; sketch strategies that will move them toward their vision; and define exactly who will take responsibility for which immediate next steps. *PATH* complements other approaches to person-centered planning when a plan calls for the kind of change that requires creative planning and sustained collaborative action.

PATH

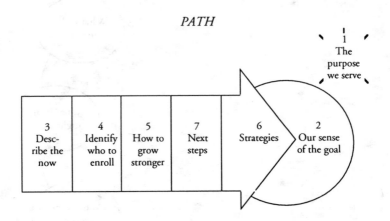

Essential Lifestyle Planning
Essential Lifestyle Planning developed from efforts to assist people
to move from institutions into community services. The process
focuses on gathering information about the focus person's core
values and preferences from the focus person and from those family
members, friends, and institution staff who know the focus person
well. This information becomes the basis for a request for proposals
from service providers and is finally incorporated into a contract
between the service system and the service provider who chooses to
assist the person. An independent agent typically directs this process. Essential Lifestyle Planning aims to provide the focus person
with a secure and effective base of service assistance.

Find out...

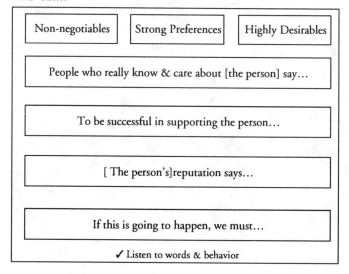

in order to......

- *Discover the person's core values & preferences*
- *Account for the person's disability & safety*
- *Develop a vision for the future*
- *Mobilize & change community services*

The future of person-centered planning

Person-centered planning can invite, align, and direct shared efforts to create positive community roles for people with disabilities. It allows people to exercise their practical wisdom to work for more inclusive, more just communities.

To support their work and its improvement, people involved in person-centered planning need to extend their network of relationships across the different approaches to person-centered planning, community development, and service reform. The future of person-centered planning depends on their willingness and ability to improve their practice through critical reflection on the effects of their work in the lives of people with disabilities and their families.

16

A Guide to Personal Futures Planning

John O'Brien

None of us makes our life alone. We each create better quality life experiences with the other people who form our social network. And usually we are resources to each other without much formal planning. Like all of us, people with severe disabilities develop in relationship. But because they rely on other people's cooperation to an unusual extent, and because human services play a larger than ordinary role in their lives, people with severe disabilities count on more able people's planning and organizing skills for assistance in identifying and meeting developmental challenges.

Personal futures planning is an orderly process for describing a desirable future with a severely disabled person and deciding on a schedule of activities and supports that will organize available resources to move toward that future. This chapter defines a perspective on good quality life experiences and describes a procedure for personal futures planning.

While it can be used to write an annual individual plan (such as an IEP or IHP), personal futures planning takes more and a different kind of effort than typical mandated individual program planning procedures. It is especially worthwhile at times when important new people enter someone's life: around transitions like going to school, moving into secondary school, leaving school, changing residence, or changing jobs; or in crisis periods. Personal futures planning is also helpful in reviewing progress and identifying new opportunities after periods of routine activity.

Personal futures planning brings together the people whose cooperation is important to a disabled person's development and focuses attention on the quality of the person's life experiences. It results in a shared sense of direction and priority which guides the selection of personal and service objectives and activities, forms the essential link between plans and action, and provides the means for regular follow-up and revision. It provides a way to get things done.

134

Those who make important decisions about another person's future need a useful vocabulary for discussing the effects of their decisions on the quality of that person's life experiences.*

This section presents a vocabulary which is helpful describing a person's situation, identifying opportunities for improvement, and evaluating the merit of proposed activities.

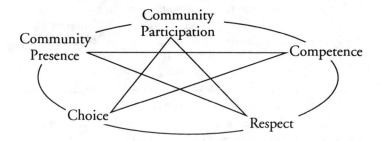

Five related terms define this way to look at the quality of a person's life experiences. Each points to experiences which it makes sense for a person to seek more of; together they indicate a balance of experiences that make effort worthwhile. History shows that people with severe disabilities are likely to miss these ordinary positive experiences unless the people they rely on work hard to provide them. These valuable experiences come from cooperation between severely disabled people and their allies. They bring out the quality of all people's lives because they are the result of personal investment, focused attention, and learning through action; they cannot

---

*The history of philosophy offers many attempts at understanding what people mean by quality of life. Each is indicative; none is definitive. In light of this history, it is presumptuous to offer any definition. But family members and service providers make decisions every day which define some aspects of life quality in action. Without some words to point to the effects of these decisions people with disabilities –whose power over decision makers is often limited to non-compliance– can easily become victims of muddled good intentions or mindless technique. This vocabulary offers a point of view on quality of life which can aid planners if they take its limitations seriously. It is based on the work of E.A. Singer as interpreted by Churchman (1982), Ackoff and Emery (1972), Emery and Emery (1976), and Gharajedaghi (1984).

be manufactured through a mechanical process. So they are identified as five essential accomplishments:[*]

- **Community Presence** is the experience of sharing the ordinary places that define community life. Without focused effort, people with severe disabilities will be separated from everyday settings by segregated facilities, activities, and schedules. Valuable activities increase the number and variety of ordinary places which a person knows and can use.

- **Choice** is the experience of growing autonomy in both small, everyday matters (like what to eat or what to wear) and large, life-defining matters (like who to live with or what sort of work to do). Personal choice defines and expresses individual identity. Without focused effort to increase available options, people with severe disabilities will be passive and without voice or the ability to exit undesirable situations. Severely disabled people can challenge other's ability to detect personal preferences. Some people may be judged incompetent to make some important decisions and rely on a guardian to choose in their interest. Valuable activities increase the variety and significance of the choices that a person makes.

- **Competence** is the experience of growing ability to skillfully perform functional and meaningful activities with whatever assistance is required. Without focused effort, people with severe disabilities will be deprived of the expectations, opportunities, instruction, and assistance necessary for development. Valued activities will increase a person's power to define and pursue objectives which are personally and socially important.

- **Respect** is the experience of having a valued place among a network of people and valued roles in community life. Without focused effort, people with severe disabilities will be confined to a narrow range of stereotyped, low status community roles which will restrict their opportunities to be seen and valued as individuals. Valuable activities will challenge limiting, negative stereotypes about a person and provide access to valued roles.

---

[*]The concept of accomplishment as the foundation for design of organizational goals is presented in Gilbert (1978). Taken together the five accomplishments described here are a definition of the principle of normalization. Complementary definitions of this fundamental principle are found in Wolfensberger and Glenn (1975), Wolfensberger and Thomas (1983), and O'Brien and Tyne (1981).

- **Community Participation** is the experience of being part of a growing network of personal relationships which includes close friends. Without focused effort, people with severe disabilities will have unusually small social networks whose membership is restricted to clients and staff of the services they use and perhaps immediate family members; many of these contacts will be impersonal and temporary. As a means to increased community participation, it is important to provide opportunities for non-disabled community members to meet and know people with severe disabilities as individuals. And necessary assistance should be provided in ways that support existing and growing relationships. Too many crucial services cut ordinary people off from relationships with severely disabled people. Valued activities will provide active opportunities for a person to meet a variety of people and develop a variety of kinds of relationships with an increasing number of people.

Each accomplishment is closely linked to the other four; each accomplishment facilitates or impairs every other. For example, a person will develop greater competence if necessary assistance and instruction are anchored in ordinary community settings and if a number of personally involved others who have overcome stereotyped perceptions are involved with the person in discovering meaningful opportunities for expression of individual interest.

Accomplishments also constrain each other. If I want to improve my competence as a marathon runner, I will have to limit some of my present preferences about schedule, diet, and tolerance for personal discomfort. At least in the short run, this will be costly to my habitual choices. The balance among competing accomplishments has to be debated and decided on the basis of each person's unique interests.

Increasing these positive experiences in a person's life means organizing three kinds of change: change in the person, change in the services that support the person, and change in the pattern of community norms and opportunities.

This set of accomplishments frames the basic question of personal futures planning:

> *"How can we identify constructive actions which will improve the quality of life experiences for the person we are concerned about? That is, how can we increase the person's experience of community presence, choice, competence, respect, and community participation?"*

A procedure for personal futures planning*

The personal futures planning process contributes to improving the quality of a person's life experiences by involving important people in describing a desirable future for the focal person and agreeing on constructive actions. This section outlines the four activities in the personal futures planning process: convening the planning group, preparing a review of the focal person's situation for the planning meeting, conducting the meeting, and following up on the implementation of the plan.

Convening the planning process

The goal of the personal futures planning process is to develop agreement on direction and priorities for constructive action among the people whose cooperation will create the focal person's future. It is important to convene the meeting in a way that includes as many of these people as possible. This means taking extra time to identify them and negotiate for their involvement.

The personal futures planning process begins with the decision that its potential benefits are worth the time and effort involved. The best way to find out what the process can offer is to try it out. An organizational trial works best if at least two or three staff people get support from their management and commit themselves to follow this outline for two or three people who rely on them. Successful personal futures planning meetings have been initiated by parents as well as service providers. The only essentials are the person's (or guardian's) consent and the commitment of time and energy. Although personal futures planning meetings have proven helpful in organizing response to a crisis situation, it makes sense to

---

*The procedure described here has been developed over the past four years by a number of practitioners who share a common perspective on quality and a common dissatisfaction with most individual program planning methods. The present state of its application is best reflected in Beth Mount's (1987) work, from which this section draws freely. Karen Green-McGowan and Mary Kovacs (1984) and Marcie Brost and Terri Johnson (1982) have also written helpful planning guides which have influenced this discussion. The format presented here is adapted from the design for the Search Conference (Williams, 1982), a method for interactive planning (O'Brien, Lyle O'Brien, and Sibbet, 1982). For a very useful treatment of techniques for personal planning see Bolles (1985), Bolles (1981), and Crystal and Bolles (1974).

learn by starting in less urgent circumstances. It's also a good idea not to start with the person who poses the most complex and challenging problems. A person who is facing an important transition is a good candidate for a first effort at personal futures planning. So is a person who has been involved in a program routine for a long time.

The purpose of convening the planning process is to actively involve the important people in the focal person's life. These are the tasks involved:

1. Develop a brief explanation of the personal futures planning process and your reasons for wanting to involve the focal person.

2. Decide on timing. It's usually best to schedule a personal futures planning meeting before the annual individual plan is due. Annual planning meetings can be completed after a personal futures planning meeting, but the two meetings should be distinct.

3. Explain the process to the focal person (and the person's guardian) and get consent for the meeting.

4. Make a list of the people who have an important role in the focal person's future and decide who to invite. Successful personal futures planning meetings have been held with as few as five and as many twenty participants. The number of people invited depends on how many people's cooperation is important to the focal person's future and on the group facilitation skills available to the meeting. Consider family members, people who have an important connection to the person's family such as friends or the family's pastor, direct service workers, other workers who may have an important relationship with the person such as a food service worker or a janitor, and the usual members of a person's individual planning team. The more your invitations bridge the usual boundaries between programs and between professionals and ordinary people the better. As you contact people, ask who else should be involved in the meeting and revise the list. If someone is unable to come to the meeting, see if they will help in describing the person's situation and whether they would like a copy of the meeting record.

5. Decide on a time and place for the planning meeting that offers the best opportunity to involve people. Plan on two to four hours for the meeting. Be sure to allow enough time to prepare for the meeting. If more than one agency is involved, think

carefully about the messages you send by the choice of a meeting place and time. Sometimes it's best to meet on neutral ground, like a church hall or library meeting room. If your history of cooperation with other important participants has been poor, it may make sense to defer to them in setting the meeting time or place. Many families appreciate service workers' willingness to meet in a way that is familiar and convenient for them. Meeting arrangements should signal that it is something outside ordinary routine.

6. Assign roles for the rest of the personal futures planning process. Who will invite people? (Remember that some people may be the key to others' active involvement; involve and enlist them in inviting others.) Who will arrange the meeting place? Who will be responsible for introducing the focal person's situation to the meeting? Who will facilitate the meeting? Who will prepare and distribute the record of the meeting?

7. Invite people to participate. Re-negotiate time and place as necessary.

8. Arrange any special accommodation or assistance the focal person needs in order to attend the meeting.

9. Anyone invited to the meeting who has not recently spent time with the focal person should do so.

Reviewing the focal person's situation

The personal futures planning meeting brings together the significant people in a severely disabled person's life for a structured discussion of the person's future. The key to success in this discussion is a well organized review of the quality of the focal person's current life experiences.

This review is different from a clinical evaluation of the person. The aim is to describe the quality of the person's present relationship to neighborhood and community people and places rather than to figure out causes for deficiencies in the person. The review supports social problem solving to increase opportunities rather than the selection of the most effective intervention to remediate the person's problems. This is not to downgrade clinical skill but to recognize its limits. If you have a good reason to believe that the focal person will benefit from clinical evaluation by one or many professional disciplines, arrange for it and decide whether or not to go ahead with the personal futures planning meeting before the results are in.

The purpose of this review is to prepare a clear and helpful introduction of the person's present situation which will assist the planning group in identifying opportunities for better quality life experiences with the focal person. The five essential accomplishments defined above provide the framework for conducting the review.

These are the tasks for the person who has agreed to introduce the person's situation to the planning meeting.

1. Begin by spending some time with the focal person. If you usually see the person in a classroom, visit at home or go out for a meal. If you are usually with the person in a group, spend some time alone together. If you live with the person, spend some time during the day. The purpose is not to assess the person or evaluate services. It is to focus your own attention on the person's situation and to signal to the person and others that "something different is happening."

2. Use the guide in the following section to describe the quality of the person's present experiences by interviewing the person and some of the important people in the person's life. Asking people to consider these questions about the person's situation is a helpful warm-up for the meeting. Challenge yourself to get as much information as possible from the focal person.

3. Prepare a summary of your findings about the quality of the person's present life experiences and decide how you will present them to the personal futures planning meeting. Some of the patterns of a person's relationship to places and people are most clearly expressed using simple diagrams. It will help focus the planning meeting's attention if you use newsprint and colored waterbased markers to make big displays to hang on the meeting room wall.

4. Review the summary with the person and with parents or others who are closest to the person. See how the person and others involved can participate in presenting the review to the planning meeting.

5. See if the focal person and parents or another close person want to make an introductory statement about what they expect from the personal futures planning meeting. If necessary help the person prepare the statement.

Guide for Review of the Quality of A Person's Life Experiences

Community Presence

- Identify the community settings the person uses regularly (daily, weekly, occasionally).
- Which of these places does the person go alone, as part of a group of two or three, or as part of a larger group?
- Does the person have any significant problem using any of these places?
- What other community settings would it be in the person's interest to use, or to use more frequently and more independently?
- What would it take to increase the number of community settings the person uses competently? (Consider changes in the person's skills, changes in available assistance, negotiating changes in the setting, or changes in service patterns.)

Choice

- Identify the daily, weekly, and occasional decisions the person makes and identify the decisions that are made for the person by others.
- Identify the person's strongest interests and the personal preferences that make the person unique.
- What would it take to increase the number, variety, and importance of the decisions the person makes?
- What would it take to increase other's knowledge of the person's interests and preferences?

Respect

- Identify the valued community roles the person occupies and the proportion of time spent in each.
- Which community roles offer the person the best opportunity to express individual gifts and talents?
- What would it take to increase the amount of time the person spends in a valued community role; in roles that express the person best?
- What images and ideas about a desirable future are available to the person?
- Does the person display any characteristics which reinforce stereotyped perceptions of people with severe disabilities?
- Are there any characteristics of the person's environment which

reinforce stereotyped perceptions of people with severe disabilities (think about the image projected by activities, schedules, expectations, and the way the person is spoken to or about).
- What would it take to decrease the stigma the person experiences?

Community Participation
- Identify the people the person spends the most time with on a daily and weekly basis. How many of these people are other clients/students in the same program? How many are program staff? How many are people without disabilities?
- Identify other important people in the person's social network with whom the person spends time occasionally.
- Identify the people who are the person's friends and allies. Who knows the person intimately? Who will advocate for the person's interests?
- What would it take to provide better support for the person's present network of relationships?
- If the person has very few friends or allies, what would it take to change the situation?
- What would it take to increase the number of non-disabled people, including age peers, who know and spend time with the person as an individual?
- What images and ideas about a desirable future are available to the person?

Competence
- Identify the competencies the person has developed during the past year. What strategies for instruction and assistance have been most effective?
- What skills could the person develop that would offer the most opportunity for increased presence, choice, respect, and participation? Are there more efficient strategies than instruction such as environmental modification or provision of additional personal assistance?
- Are there any health related threats to the person's continuing development? If so, how can these be managed effectively with minimal disruption of good quality life experiences?
- What would it take to increase the person's competence to enjoy good quality life experiences?

Use this guide to plan your review. Questions need to be individualized to fit the focal person's chronological age. When reviewing a young child's situation, it makes sense to consider the child and family together as the focus of inquiry. It isn't always necessary to answer every question; what is important is that you arrive at the planning meeting with a brief, well organized, accurate description of the person's present quality of life experiences.

It can be sobering, even painful, to make an accurate description of the quality of a severely disabled person's life experiences. Some people have very few relationships and demonstrate very limited competence, especially adults with a long history of institutionalization. Others' lives have been limited by services' failure to attend to the importance of simple, positive experiences or provide good support. In these circumstances, the personal futures planning process will be ineffective unless people cooperate in reorienting program missions to support good quality experiences. Individual planning can guide agency management but it cannot substitute for it.

Sometimes a person that others find it extremely difficult to understand has no one close enough to interpret and speak up for personal interests. This will show up in a very limited network of relationships and a poverty of information about the person's uniqueness, strengths, and interests. Lack of contact and personal information may be justified with devaluing, self-defeating statements like, "She's too low functioning to have any interests," or "His behavior is so severe no one can get near him." If someone lacks even one spokesperson who has spent enough time to form a personal relationship, the personal futures planning meeting isn't really necessary. The highest priority need has already been identified. A more elaborate meeting can await implementation of a plan to bring at least one capable and interested other person close to the focus person.

Conducting the planning meeting

Participants in a personal futures planning meeting search for a common vision of a desirable future with the focal person and identify ways to use their vision to guide everyday action. There are five parts to the meeting: reviewing the quality of the person's present life experiences; describing a desirable future for the person; selecting activities and supports which will move the person and important others into that future; and defining any necessary changes in the capability of the service system.

Roles. There are three kinds of work to be done in a successful personal futures planning meeting. Most participants should be free to focus their complete attention on describing a positive future and defining the way to get there. The group should have a clear, accurate record of its discussion and decisions. And, the group needs its work organized and managed. Unless a group is small and skillful at working together it makes sense to formally assign the tasks of facilitating and recording the meeting to people who are not central in the focal person's life.*

Before the meeting. The meeting will be successful if participants are comfortable and un-distracted. Arrange chairs so that people can see one another and the written record of the meeting. Put up the posters that summarize the review. Make posters of the ground rules and the agenda. Arrange a place for busy participants to check their beepers and provide juice, coffee, and tea.

Design of the meeting. The personal futures planning meeting moves from identification of opportunities to strategies for realizing opportunities to constructive actions. Orient participants to the structure and hold to the sequence of questions that define the agenda even though this will frustrate participants who want to jump to define solutions without exploring opportunities.

Ground rules. The facilitator should get the group's agreement to enforce these ground rules:

- We have all agreed to be here for the scheduled time. The facilitator will keep the meeting on track and adjourn at the agreed upon time.
- Everyone should be active as a listener and as a speaker. Each of us agrees to avoid disrespectful behavior like ignoring another's contribution because the person is "only a parent' or "not a family member" or using jargon without explanation.
- The focus of the meeting is on a desirable future for this person; we will carefully note barriers to attaining a desirable future but that will not compromise our appreciation of the person. In

---

*Good skills in facilitating and recording are essential to the success of any planning process. For one useful discussion of the way to build these skills see Doyle and Strauss (1976). Information on organizing meeting space, defining and managing the agenda, balancing participation, dealing with conflict, and making an accurate record is available there and will not be repeated here.

particular we will not blame the person for environmental deficiencies or for others' lack of ability and we will not avoid searching for present opportunities by defining hurdles the focal person has to jump in order to become ready for good experiences .

- We agree not to block our search with clichés (like "the community just isn't ready"), gripes that are unrelated to the focal person's future, or past resentments.

- We may disagree about many things during this meeting and no one should hold back from commenting on disagreements. But the focus of our meeting is on finding constructive things that we want to do together. So we will note disagreements but we will not try to resolve them here. Instead we will look past our real disagreements for things that we do want to do.

- We could find ourselves stuck because we lack the imagination to complete one of the agenda tasks in a constructive way. If this happens we will consider adjourning to another agreed time to make a new start on the situation.

- This meeting has no authority to require anyone to do anything. But it does offer the invitation for us to commit ourselves to new actions with the focal person. No one should make any commitment without the firm intention to honor the person by carrying it out.

Some groups have found it helpful to write the groundrules up in their own words and review them with people as they are invited.

Agenda. The two purposes of the personal futures planning meeting are to identify opportunities for better quality life experiences for the focal person and to decide on a strategy for accomplishing them. Once you are sure that participants know one another, set the ground rules, and make time for any statements of expectations, the meeting is organized by this sequence of questions:

1. What is the quality of the focal person's present life experiences?

    The person(s) responsible for summarizing the review briefly present the most important findings. The rest of the participants may add further necessary information.

2. What is changing for the person or in the surrounding environment that is likely to influence the quality of the focal person's life?

    Participants identify forces that are likely to influence the focal person's situation positively or negatively. Include both events close to the focal person, like upcoming school graduation or the deteriorating health of a family caretaker, events in the service field, like the development of a possibly useful communication system or the planned opening of a supported employment program, and events that may change the neighborhood or community, like the development of cooperative housing. Look at forces that may become important in the long term (perhaps up to five years ahead) as well as immediate influences. Identify the forces that are most likely to strongly effect the person's future. These are the events that will be worth watching and preparing for a constructive reaction.

3. What are the most important threats to the person's quality of life and opportunities for better quality life experiences for the focal person?

Considering both the person's present situation and the influencing forces, the group identifies threats —situations that will decrease the quality of the person's life experiences if no effective action is taken— and opportunities —situations where focused effort is likely to result in better quality life experiences.

4. What is our image of a desirable future for the focal person ?

Group members share their images of what life would be like for the focal person and themselves if cooperative effort results in effective action to protect against identified threats and make the most of opportunities. This is not an exercise in groundless day dreaming but a powerful tool for summarizing the direction emerging from the discussion. The more vivid the images the better. When the group's images are displayed, the first phase of the meeting is over. Take a short break.

5. What are the most critical barriers to our moving toward the desirable future we have described?

There are always at least a hundred reasons for inaction toward any worthwhile goal, but this is not the time to list them. Participants identify critical barriers —areas where concentrated action is likely to pay off. Look for barriers first in the areas where group members have most control: the pattern of support and activity offered by the service system. A group that assigns all control of the future to outside actors (such as an unwilling community or an under-financed service system), or makes the focal person the only subject of change isn't ready to move from identifying problems to taking action. If the group gets stuck at this point, reconsider the images of a desirable future. If participants ratify the images but are still stuck, it may be best to recess the meeting to allow time for reflection. Always set a definite time to reconvene and finish the meeting.

6. How will we most effectively manage these critical barriers and move toward the future we've defined?

Participants develop a strategy for improving the focal person's access to good experiences. At this point it is especially important to define ways concerned people can collaborate across the organizational or professional boundaries that too often fragment action. The strategy should clearly indicate an agreed direction. If participants cannot commit to a pattern of cooperative action which promises at least a small step toward real benefits, it is best to adjourn the meeting without pushing a make believe solution. Plans without personal commitments to action are likely to translate into a failure for the focal person ("We planned to look for a community work experience, but it never happened. It just isn't realistic for him.").

7. What are the next steps?

It's critical that someone commit to at least one change with the person that clearly reflects the images of a desirable future the group has generated. More meetings to plan may be important, but they are a poor substitute for new experiences. Participants define specific actions for the next 30 days, negotiate commitments to times and places, and agree on a mechanism for follow up.

8. Based on our discussion, do we want to make any statements about necessary changes in the service system ?

Service practices can pose very significant barriers to good experiences for people with disabilities. Participants consider actions that will inform decision makers about the undesirable effects of present policy or practice or about the importance of developing new capacities.

Follow-up

In most human services, as in many self-improvement plans, patterns of routine undermine efforts to improve quality. Unless participants in the personal futures planning meeting make small changes in daily routine based on the meeting its effects will evaporate into a vaguely pleasant memory.

Shortly after the meeting each participant receives a written record of the whole meeting, including copies of the posters summarizing the person's situation. The easiest way to prepare a useful summary of the meeting is to copy the big sheets of newsprint used to record the discussion. This provides an informal, personal summary for the people who attended. If a more formal narrative is important for the focal person's record it should be prepared separately.

Two weeks after the personal futures planning meeting the people directly responsible for managing the focal person's schedule meet briefly to review the person's last two weeks in light of the direction they set at the meeting. Naturally, this meeting includes the person, especially when limits on the person's communication make others question the person's understanding or interest. They consider the type, the number, and the balance of activities the person is involved in as well as the way the person presently performs the activities. These questions can help:

- Are there any activities in the person's schedule that are irrelevant to the direction we set together?
- Are there any activities now in the person's schedule that would be more relevant to the direction set by the plan? Are there any new activities we should develop?
- Are there any ways we could modify the way the person does scheduled activities that would lead to better quality life experiences? For example:
  - What would it take for us to increase the variety of places the person uses and the number of places the person uses alone?
  - What would it take for us to increase the amount of personal choice the person makes in pursuing these activities?
  - What would it take to increase the person's competence within these activities?
  - What would it take to improve the person's status as the person performs these activities?
  - What would it take to increase the number of personal contacts the person makes with non-disabled people through these activities?

Using the "what would it take" form for these questions separates the identification of improvements from an evaluation of the cost of making them. Once the follow-up group has made a list of potential schedule improvements, the group can decide which are worth the cost of making.

One month after the personal futures planning meeting, the person who convened the planning process should review the commitments that were made during the "Next Steps" part of the meeting by either gathering the people who accepted responsibility for action or contacting each person individually. The purpose of this check-in is to share what has happened, what has been working well, and what needs improvement.

Conclusion

Personal futures planning offers an opportunity for the people who care about a person with a severe disability to improve their understanding of the person's situation and agree on cooperative actions which will build a better future. It demands personal investment disciplined attention, and creative action. It offers better quality life experiences.

References

Ackoff, R. & Emery, F. (1972). *On purposeful systems*. London: Tavistock.

Bolles, R. (1985). *What color is your parachute? A practical guide for job hunters*. Berkeley, CA: Ten Speed Press. (This very popular book first appeared in 1972; since 1976 it is revised annually.)

Bolles, R. (1981). *The three boxes of life: A guide to life planning*. Berkeley, CA: Ten Speed Press.

Brost, M. & Johnson, T. (1982). *Getting to know you*. Madison: Wisconsin Coalition for Advocacy.

Churchman, C. W. (1982). *Thought and wisdom*. Seaside, CA: Intersystems Publications: The Systems Inquiry Series.

Crystal, J. & Bolles, R. (1980) *Where do l go from here with my life?* Berkeley, CA: Ten Speed Press.

Doyle, M. & Strauss, D. (1976). *How to make meetings work*. Chicago: Playboy Press.

Emery, F. & Emery. M. (1976). *A choice of futures*. Linden, The Netherlands: Nijhoff International Series on the Quality of Working Life, Vol. 4.

Gharajedaghi, J. (1984). On the nature of development. *Human Systems Management 4:* 163-170.

Gilbert, T. (1978). *Human competence.* New York: McGraw Hill.

Green-McGowan, K. & Kovacs, M. (1984). Twenty-four hour planning for persons with complex needs. *The Canadian Journal on Mental Retardation 34*, 1: 3-11.

Mount, B. (1987). *Personal futures planning: Finding directions for change.* Unpublished DPA dissertation, University of Georgia.

O'Brien, J., Lyle O'Brien, C. & Sibbet, D. (1982). *Planning together.* Fairbanks, AK: Governor's Council on the Handicapped and Gifted.

O'Brien, J. & Tyne, A. *(1981). The principle of normalization: A foundation for effective service.* London: Campaign for Mentally Handicapped People.

Williams, T. (1982). *Learning to manage our futures.* New York: Wiley.

Wolfensberger, W. & Glenn, L. (1975). *PASS 3.* Toronto: National Institute on Mental Retardation.

Wolfensberger, W. & Thomas, S. (1981). *PASSING: Program analysis of service systems implementing normalization goals (2nd Edition)* Toronto: National Institute on Mental Retardation.

Resources

*Personal Futures Planning**

Angela Novak Amado & Patrick Lyon (1992). *"Listen, lady, this is my life": A book of stories about personal futures planning in Minnesota*. St Paul, MN: Governor's Council of Developmental Disabilities.

Ducharme, G., Beeman, P., DeMarasse, R. & Ludlum, C. (1994). Building community one person at a time. In V. Bradley, J. Ashbaugh & B. Blaney. *Creating individual supports for people with developmental disabilities*. Baltimore, MD: Paul Brookes Publishing. Pp. 347–360.

Susannah Joyce (1993). *Collage: Stories of a circle of support*. London, ON: Realizations.

Susannah Joyce (1996). *Samplings: Seven stories of personal planning*. London, ON: Realizations.

Susannah Joyce: (1997) *Planning on... a resource book for facilitators*. London, ON: Realizations.

Beth Mount (1987). *Personal futures planning: Finding directions for change*. Unpublished DPA dissertation, University of Georgia. *Dissertation Abstracts* Accession number AAG8724642 (Copies available from Graphic Futures)

Beth Mount (1989). *Making futures happen: A manual for facilitators of personal futures planning*. St Paul, MN: Governor's Council on Developmental Disabilities.

Beth Mount (1990). *Imperfect change: Embracing the tensions of person-centered work*. Manchester, CT: Communitas.

Beth Mount (1991). *Dare to dream: An analysis of the conditions leading to personal change for people with disabilities*. Manchester, CT: Communitas.

Beth Mount (1995). *Capacity works: Finding windows for change using personal futures planning*. Manchester, CT: Communitas.

---

*Note: Some people call this approach "lifestyle planning," probably because copies of O'Brien's chapter by that name (1987) were widely circulated. This chapter was written about personal futures planning, which was re-named lifestyle planning by the book's editors in the context of its application to the activities catalog approach to school curriculum development.

Beth Mount (1997). *Finding directions for change using personal futures planning: A sourcebook of values, ideas, & methods.* New York: Graphic Futures.

Beth Mount, George Ducharme, & Pat Beeman (1991). *Person-centered development: A journey in learning to listen to people with disabilities.* Manchester, CT: Communitas.

Beth Mount & Kay Zwernick (1988). *It's never too early, Its never too late: An overview of personal futures planning.* St Paul, MN: Governor's Council on Developmental Disabilities.

John O'Brien (1987). A guide to lifestyle planning. In B. Wilcox & T. Bellamy, Eds. *A Comprehensive guide to the activities catalog.* Baltimore, MD: Paul Brookes Publishing Co.

John O'Brien, Beth Mount, & Connie Lyle O'Brien (1990). *The personal profile.* Lithonia, GA: Responsive Systems Associates.

Jack Pealer & Sandra Landis (1990) *What have we noticed as we have tried to assist people one person at a time.* Chillicothe, OH: Ohio Safeguards.

Jack Pealer & Sandra Landis (1990). *Suggestions for exploring and recording the personal history of someone we're assisting to plan.* Chillicothe, OH: Ohio Safeguards.

CONTACT:

Communitas • Box 374 • Manchester, CT 06040

Graphic Futures • 25 West 81st St, 16-B • New York, NY 10024

MN Governor's Planning Council on Developmental Disabilities • Centennial Office Building • St Paul, MN 55155

Ohio Safeguards • PO Box 1943 • Chillicothe, OH 45601

Realizations • PO Box 1430, Station B • London, ON N6A 5M2

Responsive Systems Associates • 58 Willowick Dr • Lithonia, GA 30038

Individual Service Design

Lovett, H. (1996). *Learning to listen: Positive approaches and people with difficult behavior.* Baltimore, MD: Paul Brookes Publishing.

Jack Yates (1980). *Program design sessions.* Carver, MA: Author.

CONTACT

Jack Yates • DMR Region 5 • 500 Main St • Carver, MA 02072

Essential Lifestyle Planning

Michael Smull & Susan Burke Harrison (1992). *Supporting people with severe reputations in the community.* Alexandria, VA: NASMRPD.

Michael Smull (1997) *A blueprint for essential lifestyle planning.* Napa: CA: Allen, Shea & Associate

Michael Smull, Helen Sanderson & Susan Burke Harrison, (1996). *Reviewing essential lifestyle plans: Crietria for best plans.* Kenisington, MD: Support Development Associates.

These and a variety of other helpful papers by Michael Smull and his colleagues can be found on the Allen, Shea & Associates web page: www.napanet.net/business/personal/ASA

CONTACT:

Michael Smull • Support Development Associates 4208 Knowles • Kensington, MD 20895

NASMRPD • 113 Oronoco St • Alexandria, VA 22314

MAPS & PATH

John O'Brien & Marsha Forest. (1989). *Action for inclusion.* Toronto: Inclusion Press.

Jack Pearpoint, John O'Brien, & Marsha Forest. (1995) *PATH (Second Edition).* Toronto: Inclusion Press

Judith Snow. *What's really worth doing? & How to do it.* Toronto: Inclusion Press.

Jack Pearpoint (1990). *From behind the piano: The building of Judith Snow's unique circle of friends.* Toronto: Inclusion Press.

Inclusion Press distributes a set of video training tapes on both *MAPS* and *PATH* including *The New MAPS Training Video, The PATH Training Video* and *PATH in Action.* .

Karen Green (1984). Twenty-four hour planning for persons with complex needs. *Canadian Journal on Mental Retardation 34,* 1, 3-11.

Falvey, M. Forest, M., Pearpoint, J. & Rosenberg, R. (Second Edition) (1998). *All my life's a circle: Using the tools – Circles, MAPS and PATH.* Toronto: Inclusion Press.

154

Marsha Forest & Evelyn Lusthaus (1989). Promoting educational equality for all students: Circles and MAPS. In S. Stainback, W. Stainback, & M. Forest. *Educating all students in the mainstream of regular education.* Baltimore, MD: Paul Brookes Publishing Co. pp. 43-57.

Marsha Forest & Jack Pearpoint (1992). Commonsense tools: MAPS and circles. In J. Pearpoint, M. Forest, & J. Snow, Eds. *The inclusion papers: Strategies to make inclusion work.* Toronto: Inclusion Press, pp. 52-57.

CONTACT
Inclusion Press • 24 Thome Cres. • Toronto, ON M6H 2S5
www.inclusion.com

Person-centered planning and organizational change

Helen Sanderson, Jo Kennedy & Pete Richie. (1997). *People, plans & possibilities: Exploring person-centered planning.* Edinburgh: SHS, Ltd.

CONTACT
SHS, Ltd • 1a Washintgton Court, Washington Lane • Edinburgh, Scotland EH11 2HA

INCLUSION PRESS ORDER FORM

24 Thorne Crescent, Toronto, ON Canada M6H 2S5
Tel: 416-658-5363 Fax: 416-658-5067
E-mail: inclusionpress@inclusion.com WEB: http://www.inclusion.com

Inclusion SPECIAL PACKS...   [** = new products]

ll Means All PACK	$110 + $10 shipping/pack	
- Video: All Means All, plus & book: All My Life's a Circle		
he Community PACK	$ 40 + $7 shipping/pack	
- Members of Each Other & Celebrating the Ordinary - 2 books - John O'Brien & Connie Lyle O'Brien		
he Education Book PACK	$ 40 + $7 shipping/pack	
- Inclusion: Recent Research & Inclusion: How To - 2 Books - Gary Bunch		
riendship PACK (1 book + Video)	$ 60 + $10 shipping/pack	
- [Friendship Video + From Behind the Piano/What's Really Worth Doing]		
clusion Classics Book PACK [Action for Inclusion + Inclusion Papers]	$ 30 + $7 shipping/pack	
clusion Classics Videos PACK (DVD format also available)	$ 90 + $12 shipping/pack	
- Videos [With a Little Help from My Friends & Kids Belong Together]		
ATH IN ACTION PACK (DVD format also available)	$150 + $15 shipping/pack	
- 2 Path Training Videos [(Path in Action + Path Training) + Path Workbook]		
etroglyphs Pack - (book & video on inclusion in High Schools from UNH)	$ 60 + $10 shipping/pack	
PlayFair Teams Kit - (Teacher's book, Advocate's book , Intro CD, 2 posters)	$ 65 + $10 shipping/pack	
hen Spider Webs Unite PACK - Shafik Asante - Book and Video	$ 80 + $10 shipping/pack	

Books

		Copies	Total
ction for Inclusion - Classic on Inclusion	$20 + $5 /1st copy shipping		
l My Life's a Circle Expanded Edition- Circles, MAPS & PATH	$20 + $5 /1st copy shipping		
e All Star Company - Team Building by Nick Marsh	$20 + $5 /1st copy shipping		
e Careless Society - John McKnight	$25 + $5 /1st copy shipping		
elebrating the Ordinary O'Brien, O'Brien & Jacob	$25 + $5 /1st copy shipping		
rcle of Friends by Bob & Martha Perske	$25 + $5 /1st copy shipping		
ommunity Lost & Found Arthur Lockhart & Michael Clarke	$30 + $5 /1st copy shipping		
eating Circles of Friends - Colin Newton & Derek Wilson	$25 + $5 /1st copy shipping		
You Hear What I Hear? - Janice Fialka & Karen Mikus	$15 + $5 /1st copy shipping		
eam Catchers & Dolphins Marsha Forest and Jack Pearpoint	$20 + $5 /1st copy shipping		
Each Belongs (book with CD) -Jim Hansen w/Leyden, Bunch, Pearpoint	$30 + $5 /1st copy shipping		
Free to Fly, A Story of Manic Depression -Caroline Fei-Yeng Kwok	$25+ $5 /1st copy shipping		
om Behind the Piano, by Jack Pearpoint AND **What's Really Worth Doing** by Judith Snow			
- Now in ONE Book *	$20 + $5 /1st copy shipping		
nts for Graphic Facilitators by Jack Pearpoint	$25 + $5 /1st copy shipping		
plementing Person-Centered Planning: Voices of Experience			
Edited by John O'Brien & Connie Lyle O'Brien	$25 + $5 /1st copy shipping		
e Inclusion Papers - Strategies & Stories	$20 + $5 /1st copy shipping		
clusion: How To Essential Classroom Strategies - Gary Bunch	$25+ $5 /1st copy shipping		
clusion: Recent Research G. Bunch & A. Valeo	$25 + $5 /1st copy shipping		
Matters - Lessons from my Son - Janice Fialka	$15 + $5 /1st copy shipping		
ds, Disabilities Regular Classrooms Gary Bunch	$20 + $5 /1st copy shipping		
ssons for Inclusion Curriculum Ideas for Inclusion in Elementary Schools	$20 + $5 /1st copy shipping		
Little Book About Person Centered Planning	$20 + $5 /1st copy shipping		
Forest, Lovett, Mount, Pearpoint, Smull, Snow, and Strully			
Make a Difference: Direct Support Guidebook (J. O'Brien & B Mount)	$20 + $5 shipping /1st copy		
Make a Difference: Leader's Resource Kit (Instructor's book + CD)	$30 + $5 shipping /1st copy		
Make a Difference: Learning Journey Booklet (packet of 10)	$20 + $5 shipping /1st set		
embers of Each Other John O'Brien & Connie Lyle O'Brien	$25 + $5 /1st copy shipping		
e Candle Power by Cathy Ludlum & Communitas	$25 + $5 /1st copy shipping		
th Workbook - 2nd Edition Planning Positive Possible Futures	$20 + $5 /1st copy shipping		
rske - Pencil Portraits 1971-1990	$30 + $5 /1st copy shipping		
rson-Centred Planning with MAPS & PATH			
by John O'Brien & Jack Pearpoint	$25 + $5 /1st copy shipping		
troglyphs - Inclusion in High School from UNH	$20 + $5 /1st copy shipping		
PlayFair Teams: A Manual for Teacher Advisors	$15 + $5 /1st copy shipping		
PlayFair Teams: A Community Advocate's Manual	$15 + $5 /1st copy shipping		

Item	Price		
Reflections on Inclusive Education	$15 + $5 /1st copy shipping	___	___
Restorative Justice Art Lockhart, Lynn Zammit, Randy Charboneau	$30 + $5 /1st copy shipping	___	___
**The Basics-Supporting Learners w/Intellectual Challenge-Bunch	$20 + $5 /1st copy shipping	___	___
Treasures - from UNH	$20 + $5 /1st copy shipping	___	___
Waddie Welcome & the Beloved Community T.Kohler & S.Earl	$25 + $5 /1st copy shipping	___	___
**When People Care Enough to Act (ABCD in Action)	$25 + $5 /1st copy shipping	___	___
When Spider Webs Unite Community & Inclusion- Shafik Asante	$20 + $5 /1st copy shipping	___	___
Yes! She Knows She's Here Nicola Schaefer's Book about Kathrine	$20 + $5 /1st copy shipping	___	___
Inclusion – Exclusion Poster (18 X 24)	$10 + $5 /1st copy shipping	___	___
Person Centered Direct Support Foldout (call for bulk rates)	$ 5 + $2 /1st copy shipping	___	___
Inclusion News in Bulk (box of 100)	$50 – includes shipping in NA	___	___

MEDIA: VIDEOs • CD-ROMs • DVDs

Item	Price		
ABCD in Action - DVD Mike Green & Henry Moore & John McKnight (includes book)	$150 + $8 shipping /1st copy	___	
All Means All - Inclusion Video Introduction to Circles, MAPS and PATH	$100 + $8 shipping /1st copy	___	
Dream Catchers (Dreams & Circles)	$55 + $8 shipping /1st copy	___	
Each Belongs (30 years of Inclusion-15 min. celebration in Hamilton)	$50 + $8 shipping /1st copy	___	
EVERYONE Has a GIFT John McKnight - Building Communities of Capacity	$75 + $8 shipping /1st copy	___	
**Finding Meaning in the Work - (CD + Manual) (O'Briens)	$195 + $8 shipping /1st copy	___	
Friendship Video Judith, Marsha & Jack on Friendship	$55 + $8 shipping /1st copy	___	
The Inclusion Classics - DVD (2 classic inclusion videos on DVD)	$ 90 + $8 shipping /1st copy	___	
Kids Belong Together - MAPS & Circles	$55 + $8 shipping /1st copy	___	
The MAPS Collection - DVD (2 MAPS Training videos on DVD)	$150 + $8 shipping /1st copy	___	
Miller's MAP - MAPS in Action	$55 + $8 shipping /1st copy	___	
**My Life, My Choice - DVD (7 stories of adults with full lives)	$150 + $8 shipping /1st copy	___	
NEW MAPS TRAINING Video Shafik's MAP - MAPS Process - Step by Step	$75 + $8 shipping /1st copy	___	
The PATH Collection - DVD (2 PATH Training videos on DVD)	$150 + $8 shipping /1st copy	___	
PATH Demo Video Univ of Dayton Ohio - Video of Workshop on PATH	$55 + $8 shipping /1st copy	___	
PATH IN ACTION Working with Groups -Training Video for Path with Groups	$100 + $8 shipping /1st copy	___	
PATH TRAINING Video Intro Training Video - An Individual Path (Joe's Path)	$75 + $8 shipping /1st copy	___	
Person Centered Direct Support - CD - 4 minute video & powerpoint	$ 25 + $8 shipping /1st copy	___	
Petroglyphs Video Companion to Petroglyphs Book - Packaged with book	$60 + $8 shipping /1st copy	___	
**PlayFair Teams DVD an introduction to PlayFair Teams -	$50 + $8 shipping /1st copy	___	
ReDiscovering MAPS Charting Your Journey -brand NEW MAPS training video	$100 + $8 shipping /1st copy	___	
Together We're Better (3 videos) Staff Development Kit	$175 + $12 shipping	___	
TOOLS FOR CHANGE - The CD-Rom for Person Centred Planning			
Pricing is dependent on a licensing agreement. To obtain licensing information check our website, e-mail or call us.			
When Spider Webs Unite - Video Shafik Asante in Action	$75 + $8 /1st copy shipping	___	___
With a Little Help from My Friends The Classic on Circles & MAPS	$55 + $8 /1st copy shipping	___	___

Plus applicable taxes (variable)

GRAND TOTAL $===========

New Resources:
- ABCD in Action-DVD & Book: When People Care Enough to A
- My Life My Choice - DVD - Seven Adults living full lives
- Make a Difference - book; training pack, note kit
- Each Belongs - book & CD - The 1st Inclusive School Board ever!
- PlayFair Teams - 2 books, DVD + Posters - blended teams in schools.
- Find Meaning in the Work - CD & Manual - presentation ready!
- Free to Fly - A Story of Manic Depression - Caroline Kwok
- Supporting Learners with Intellectual Challenge -teacher resources

Tools for Change

CD - Tools for Person Centered Planning

Name: _____
Organization: _____
Address: _____
City: _____
Prov/State _____ Post Code/ZIP _____
Wk Phone _____ Cheque Enclosed _____
Hm Phone _____ Fax _____
E-Mail _____ Web Page: _____

INCLUSION PRESS ORDER FORM

24 Thorne Crescent, Toronto, ON Canada M6H 2S5
Tel: 416-658-5363 Fax: 416-658-5067
E-mail: inclusionpress@inclusion.com WEB: http://www.inclusion.com

Inclusion SPECIAL PACKS...   [** = new products]

ll Means All PACK	$110 + $10 shipping/pack		
- Video: All Means All, plus & book: All My Life's a Circle			
he Community PACK	$ 40 + $7 shipping/pack		
- Members of Each Other & Celebrating the Ordinary - 2 books - John O'Brien & Connie Lyle O'Brien			
he Education Book PACK	$ 40 + $7 shipping/pack		
- Inclusion: Recent Research & Inclusion: How To - 2 Books - Gary Bunch			
riendship PACK (1 book + Video)	$ 60 + $10 shipping/pack		
- [Friendship Video + From Behind the Piano/What's Really Worth Doing]			
clusion Classics Book PACK [Action for Inclusion + Inclusion Papers]	$ 30 + $7 shipping/pack		
clusion Classics Videos PACK (DVD format also available)	$ 90 + $12 shipping/pack		
- Videos [With a Little Help from My Friends + Kids Belong Together]			
ATH IN ACTION PACK (DVD format also available)	$150 + $15 shipping/pack		
- 2 Path Training Videos [(Path in Action + Path Training) + Path Workbook]			
etroglyphs Pack - (book & video on inclusion in High Schools from UNH)	$ 60 + $10 shipping/pack		
PlayFair Teams Kit - (Teacher's book, Advocate's book , Intro CD, 2 posters)	$ 65 + $10 shipping/pack		
hen Spider Webs Unite PACK - Shafik Asante - Book and Video	$ 80 + $10 shipping/pack		

Books   Copies Total

ction for Inclusion - Classic on Inclusion	$20 + $5 /1st copy shipping		
ll My Life's a Circle Expanded Edition- Circles, MAPS & PATH	$20 + $5 /1st copy shipping		
he All Star Company - Team Building by Nick Marsh	$20 + $5 /1st copy shipping		
he Careless Society - John McKnight	$25 + $5 /1st copy shipping		
elebrating the Ordinary O'Brien, O'Brien & Jacob	$25 + $5 /1st copy shipping		
ircle of Friends by Bob & Martha Perske	$25 + $5 /1st copy shipping		
ommunity Lost & Found Arthur Lockhart & Michael Clarke	$30 + $5 /1st copy shipping		
reating Circles of Friends - Colin Newton & Derek Wilson	$25 + $5 /1st copy shipping		
o You Hear What I Hear? - Janice Fialka & Karen Mikus	$15 + $5 /1st copy shipping		
ream Catchers & Dolphins Marsha Forest and Jack Pearpoint	$20 + $5 /1st copy shipping		
Each Belongs (book with CD) -Jim Hansen w/Leyden, Bunch, Pearpoint	$30 + $5 /1st copy shipping		
Free to Fly, A Story of Manic Depression -Caroline Fei-Yeng Kwok	$25+ $5 /1st copy shipping		
om Behind the Piano, by Jack Pearpoint AND **What's Really Worth Doing** by Judith Snow			
- Now in ONE Book *	$20 + $5 /1st copy shipping		
nts for Graphic Facilitators by Jack Pearpoint	$25 + $5 /1st copy shipping		
nplementing Person-Centered Planning: Voices of Experience			
Edited by John O'Brien & Connie Lyle O'Brien	$25 + $5 /1st copy shipping		
he Inclusion Papers - Strategies & Stories	$20 + $5 /1st copy shipping		
clusion: How To Essential Classroom Strategies - Gary Bunch	$25+ $5 /1st copy shipping		
clusion: Recent Research G. Bunch & A. Valeo	$25 + $5 /1st copy shipping		
Matters - Lessons from my Son - Janice Fialka	$15 + $5 /1st copy shipping		
ds, Disabilities Regular Classrooms Gary Bunch	$20 + $5 /1st copy shipping		
essons for Inclusion Curriculum Ideas for Inclusion in Elementary Schools	$20 + $5 /1st copy shipping		
Little Book About Person Centered Planning	$20 + $5 /1st copy shipping		
Forest, Lovett, Mount, Pearpoint, Small, Snow, and Strully			
Make a Difference: Direct Support Guidebook (J. O'Brien & B Mount)	$20 + $5 shipping /1st copy		
Make a Difference: Leader's Resource Kit (Instructor's book + CD)	$30 + $5 shipping /1st copy		
Make a Difference: Learning Journey Booklet (packet of 10)	$20 + $5 shipping /1st set		
embers of Each Other John O'Brien & Connie Lyle O'Brien	$25 + $5 /1st copy shipping		
he Candle Power by Cathy Ludlum & Communitas	$25 + $5 /1st copy shipping		
th Workbook - 2nd Edition Planning Positive Possible Futures	$20 + $5 /1st copy shipping		
erske - Pencil Portraits 1971-1990	$30 + $5 /1st copy shipping		
erson-Centred Planning with MAPS & PATH			
by John O'Brien & Jack Pearpoint	$25 + $5 /1st copy shipping		
etroglyphs - Inclusion in High School from UNH	$20 + $5 /1st copy shipping		
PlayFair Teams: A Manual for Teacher Advisors	$15 + $5 /1st copy shipping		
PlayFair Teams: A Community Advocate's Manual	$15 + $5 /1st copy shipping		

Reflections on Inclusive Education	$15 + $5 /1st copy shipping	_____ _____
Restorative Justice Art Lockhart, Lynn Zammit, Randy Charboneau	$30 + $5 /1st copy shipping	_____ _____
**The Basics-Supporting Learners w/Intellectual Challenge-Bunch	$20 + $5 /1st copy shipping	_____ _____
Treasures - from UNH	$20 + $5 /1st copy shipping	_____ _____
Waddie Welcome & the Beloved Community T.Kohler & S.Earl	$25 + $5 /1st copy shipping	_____ _____
**When People Care Enough to Act (ABCD in Action)	$25 + $5 /1st copy shipping	_____ _____
When Spider Webs Unite Community & Inclusion- Shafik Asante	$20 + $5 /1st copy shipping	_____ _____
Yes! She Knows She's Here Nicola Schaefer's Book about Kathrine	$20 + $5 /1st copy shipping	_____ _____
Inclusion – Exclusion Poster (18 X 24)	$10 + $5 /1st copy shipping	_____ _____
Person Centered Direct Support Foldout (call for bulk rates)	$ 5 + $2 /1st copy shipping	_____ _____
Inclusion News in Bulk (box of 100)	$50 – includes shipping in NA	_____ _____

MEDIA: VIDEOs • CD-ROMs • DVDs

ABCD in Action - DVD Mike Green & Henry Moore & John McKnight (includes book)	$150 + $8 shipping /1st copy	_____ _____
All Means All - Inclusion Video Introduction to Circles, MAPS and PATH	$100 + $8 shipping /1st copy	_____ _____
Dream Catchers (Dreams & Circles)	$55 + $8 shipping /1st copy	_____ _____
Each Belongs (30 years of Inclusion-15 min. celebration in Hamilton)	$50 + $8 shipping /1st copy	_____ _____
EVERYONE Has a GIFT John McKnight - Building Communities of Capacity	$75 + $8 shipping /1st copy	_____ _____
**Finding Meaning in the Work - (CD + Manual) (O'Briens)	$195 + $8 shipping /1st copy	_____ _____
Friendship Video Judith, Marsha & Jack on Friendship	$55 + $8 shipping /1st copy	_____ _____
The Inclusion Classics - DVD (2 classic inclusion videos on DVD)	$ 90 + $8 shipping /1st copy	_____ _____
Kids Belong Together - MAPS & Circles	$55 + $8 shipping /1st copy	_____ _____
The MAPS Collection - DVD (2 MAPS Training videos on DVD)	$150 + $8 shipping /1st copy	_____ _____
Miller's MAP - MAPS in Action	$55 + $8 shipping /1st copy	_____ _____
**My Life, My Choice - DVD (7 stories of adults with full lives)	$150 + $8 shipping /1st copy	_____ _____
NEW MAPS TRAINING Video Shafik's MAP - MAPS Process - Step by Step	$75 + $8 shipping /1st copy	_____ _____
The PATH Collection - DVD (2 PATH Training videos on DVD)	$150 + $8 shipping /1st copy	_____ _____
PATH Demo Video Univ of Dayton Ohio - Video of Workshop on PATH	$55 + $8 shipping /1st copy	_____ _____
PATH IN ACTION Working with Groups -Training Video for Path with Groups	$100 + $8 shipping /1st copy	_____ _____
PATH TRAINING Video Intro Training Video - An Individual Path {Joe's Path}	$75 + $8 shipping /1st copy	_____ _____
Person Centered Direct Support - CD - 4 minute video & powerpoint	$ 25 + $8 shipping /1st copy	_____ _____
Petroglyphs Video Companion to Petroglyphs Book - **Packaged with book**	$60 + $8 shipping /1st copy	_____ _____
**PlayFair Teams DVD an introduction to PlayFair Teams -	$50 + $8 shipping /1st copy	_____ _____
ReDiscovering MAPS Charting Your Journey -brand NEW MAPS training video	$100 + $8 shipping /1st copy	_____ _____
Together We're Better (3 videos) Staff Development Kit	$175 + $12 shipping	_____ _____
TOOLS FOR CHANGE - The CD-Rom for Person Centred Planning		_____
Pricing is dependent on a licensing agreement. To obtain licensing information check our website, e-mail or call us.		
When Spider Webs Unite - Video Shafik Asante in Action	$75 + $8 /1st copy shipping	_____ _____
With a Little Help from My Friends The Classic on Circles & MAPS	$55 + $8 shipping /1st copy	_____ _____

Plus applicable taxes (variable)

GRAND TOTAL $===========

New Resources:
• **ABCD in Action**-DVD & Book: When People Care Enough to Ac
• **My Life My Choice** - DVD - Seven Adults living full lives
• **Make a Difference** - book; training pack, note kit
• **Each Belongs** - book & CD - The 1st Inclusive School Board ever!
• **PlayFair Teams** - 2 books, DVD + Posters - blended teams in schools.
• **Find Meaning in the Work** - CD & Manual - presentation ready!
• **Free to Fly** - A Story of Manic Depression - Caroline Kwok
• **Supporting Learners with Intellectual Challenge** -teacher resources

Tools for Change

CD Tools for
Person Centered Planning

Name: _____
Organization:_____
Address:_____
City:_____
Prov/State _____ Post Code/ZIP _____
Wk Phone _____ Cheque Enclosed _____
Hm Phone _____ Fax _____
E-Mail _____ Web Page:_____

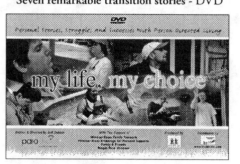